# RUNAWAYS

## DEAD WRONG



WRITER: **TERRY MOORE**
PENCILS: **HUMBERTO RAMOS**
INKS: **DAVE MEIKIS**
COLORS: **CHRISTINA STRAIN**
LETTERS: **VC's JOE CARAMAGNA**
COVER ART: **HUMBERTO RAMOS** & **CHRISTINA STRAIN**
ASSISTANT EDITOR: **DANIEL KETCHUM**
EDITOR: **NICK LOWE**

***RUNAWAYS*** CREATED BY **BRIAN K. VAUGHAN** & **ADRIAN ALPHONA**

COLLECTION EDITOR: JENNIFER GRÜNWALD
ASSISTANT EDITOR: CAITLIN O'CONNELL
ASSOCIATE MANAGING EDITOR: KATERI WOODY
EDITOR, SPECIAL PROJECTS: MARK D. BEAZLEY
VP PRODUCTION & SPECIAL PROJECTS: JEFF YOUNGQUIST
SVP PRINT, SALES & MARKETING: DAVID GABRIEL

EDITOR IN CHIEF: C.B. CEBULSKI
CHIEF CREATIVE OFFICER: JOE QUESADA
PRESIDENT: DAN BUCKLEY
EXECUTIVE PRODUCER: ALAN FINE

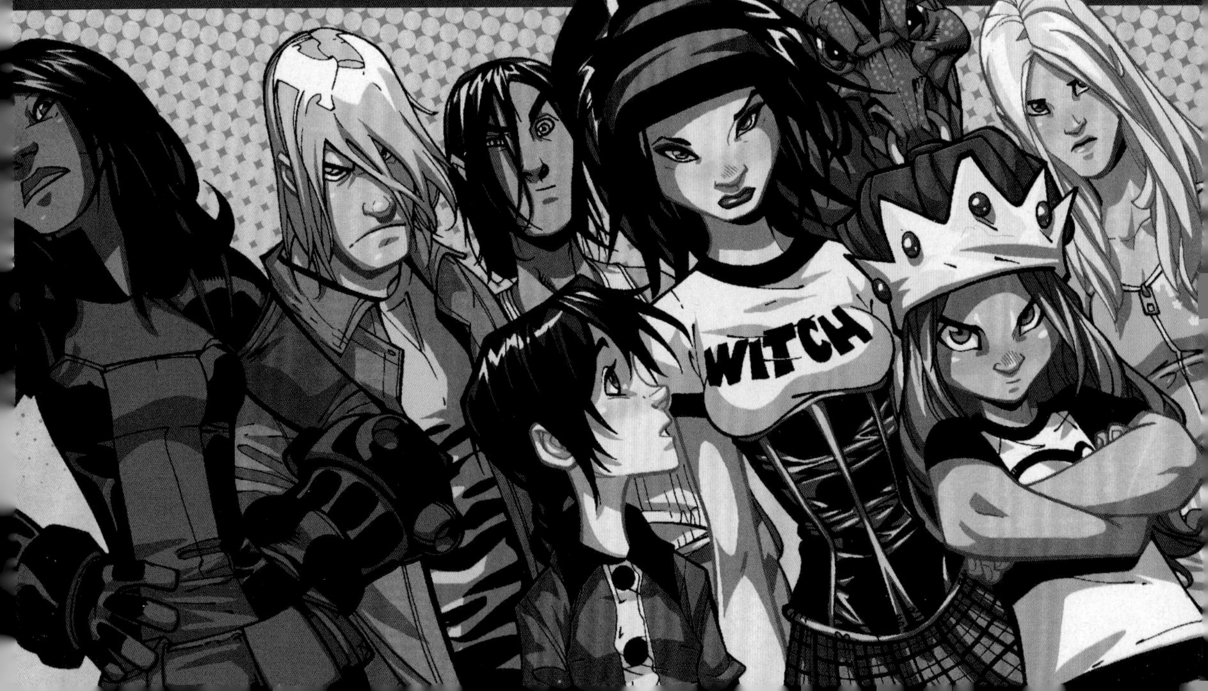
WITCH

## PREVIOUSLY:

AT SOME POINT IN THEIR LIVES, ALL KIDS THINK THAT THEIR PARENTS ARE EVIL. FOR MOLLY HAYES AND HER FRIENDS, THIS IS ESPECIALLY TRUE.

ONE NIGHT, MOLLY AND HER FRIENDS DISCOVERED THAT THEIR PARENTS WERE A GROUP OF SUPER-POWERED CRIME BOSSES WHO CALLED THEMSELVES "THE PRIDE." USING TECHNOLOGY AND RESOURCES STOLEN FROM THEIR PARENTS, THE TEENAGERS WERE ABLE TO STOP THE PRIDE AND BREAK THEIR CRIMINAL HOLD ON LOS ANGELES. BUT THEY'VE BEEN ON THE RUN ON EVER SINCE.

NOW, AFTER A FEW PERILOUS ADVENTURES IN NEW YORK CITY, NICO MINORU, CHASE STEIN, KAROLINA DEAN, MOLLY HAYES, VICTOR MANCHA, XAVIN AND KLARA ARE RETURNING TO THE CITY THEY KNOW BEST — LOS ANGELES.

**RUNAWAYS VOL. 9: DEAD WRONG.** Contains material originally published in magazine form as RUNAWAYS #1-6. Second edition. First printing 2018. ISBN 978-1-302-90910-9. Published by MARVEL WORLDWIDE, INC., a subsidiary of MARVEL ENTERTAINMENT, LLC. OFFICE OF PUBLICATION: 135 West 50th Street, New York, NY 10020. Copyright © 2018 MARVEL No similarity between any of the names, characters, persons, and/or institutions in this magazine with those of any living or dead person or institution is intended, and any such similarity which may exist is purely coincidental. **Printed in Canada.** DAN BUCKLEY, President, Marvel Entertainment; JOE QUESADA, Chief Creative Officer; TOM BREVOORT, SVP of Publishing; DAVID BOGART, SVP of Business Affairs & Operations, Publishing & Partnership; DAVID GABRIEL, SVP of Sales & Marketing, Publishing; JEFF YOUNGQUIST, VP of Production & Special Projects; DAN CARR, Executive Director of Publishing Technology; ALEX MORALES, Director of Publishing Operations; SUSAN CRESPI, Production Manager; STAN LEE, Chairman Emeritus. For information regarding advertising in Marvel Comics or on Marvel.com, please contact Vit DeBellis, Custom Solutions & Integrated Advertising Manager, at vdebellis@marvel.com. For Marvel subscription inquiries, please call 888-511-5480. **Manufactured between 12/29/2017 and 1/30/2018 by SOLISCO PRINTERS, SCOTT, QC, CANADA.**

10 9 8 7 6 5 4 3 2 1

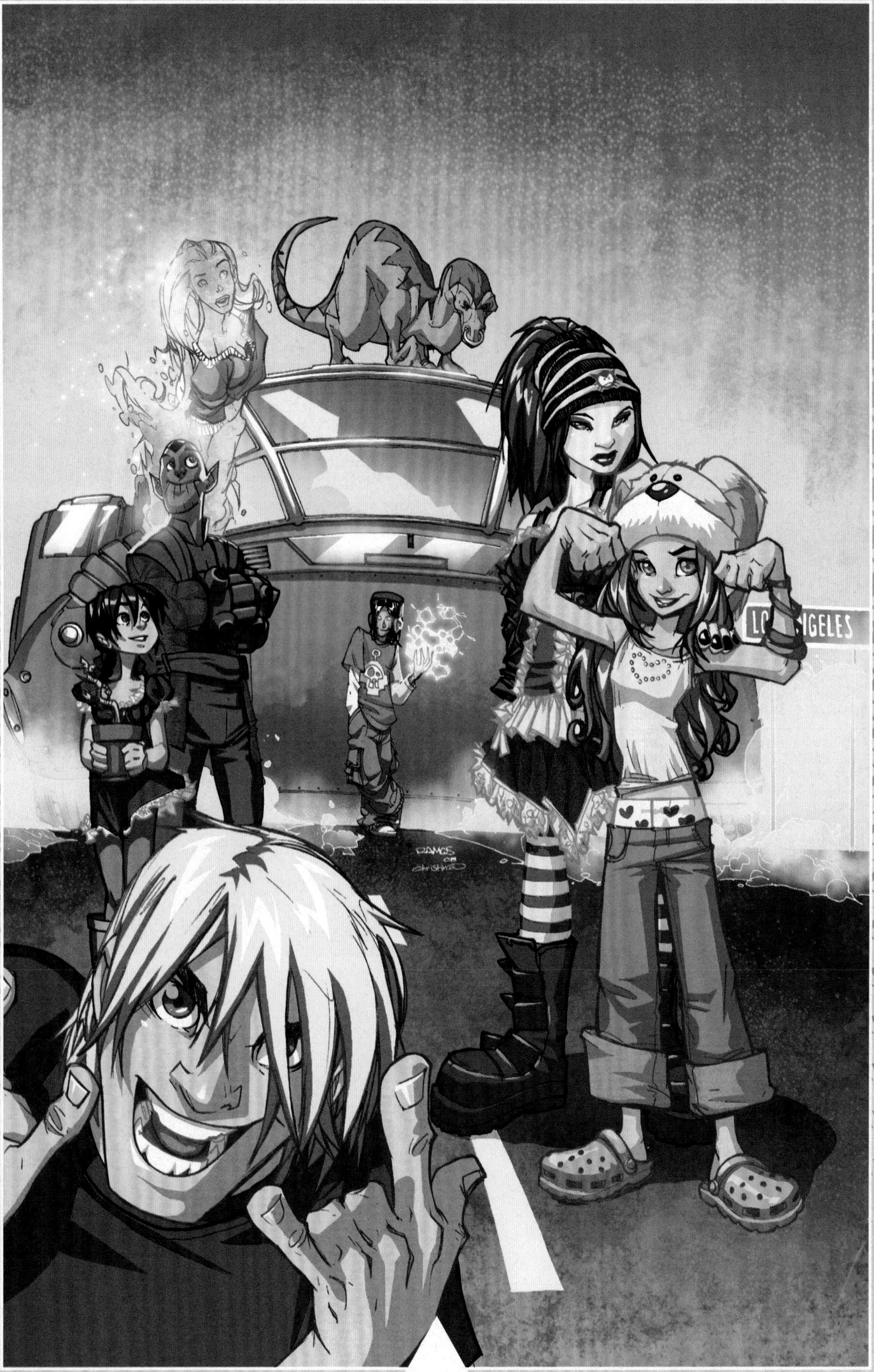
RAMOS
08

1

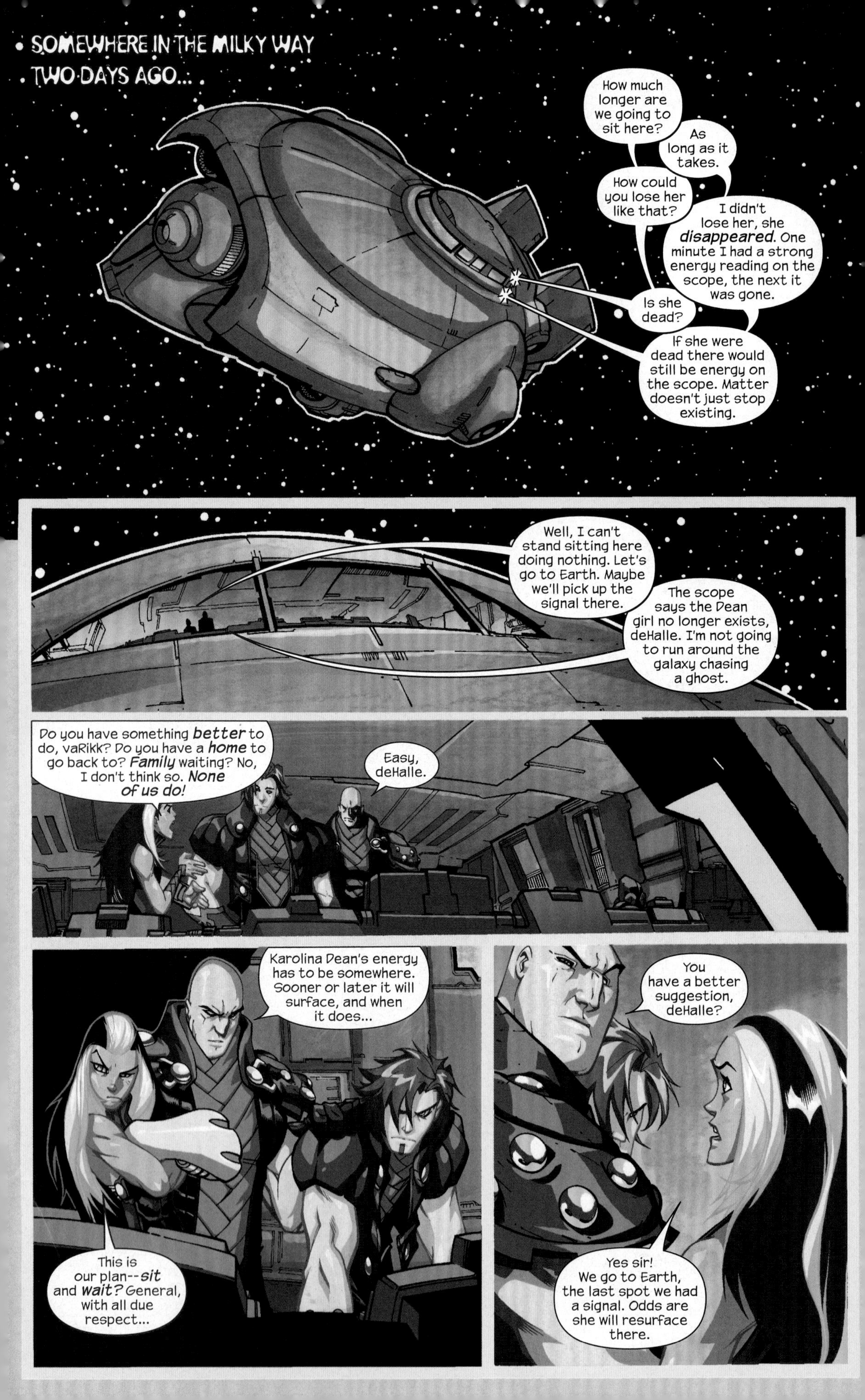
SOMEWHERE IN THE MILKY WAY
TWO DAYS AGO...
How much longer are we going to sit here?
As long as it takes.
How could you lose her like that?
I didn't lose her, she **disappeared**. One minute I had a strong energy reading on the scope, the next it was gone.
Is she dead?
If she were dead there would still be energy on the scope. Matter doesn't just stop existing.
Well, I can't stand sitting here doing nothing. Let's go to Earth. Maybe we'll pick up the signal there.
The scope says the Dean girl no longer exists, deHalle. I'm not going to run around the galaxy chasing a ghost.
Do you have something ***better*** to do, vaRikk? Do you have a ***home*** to go back to? ***Family*** waiting? No, I don't think so. ***None of us do!***
Easy, deHalle.
Karolina Dean's energy has to be somewhere. Sooner or later it will surface, and when it does...
This is our plan--***sit*** and ***wait?*** General, with all due respect...
You have a better suggestion, deHalle?
Yes sir! We go to Earth, the last spot we had a signal. Odds are she will resurface there.

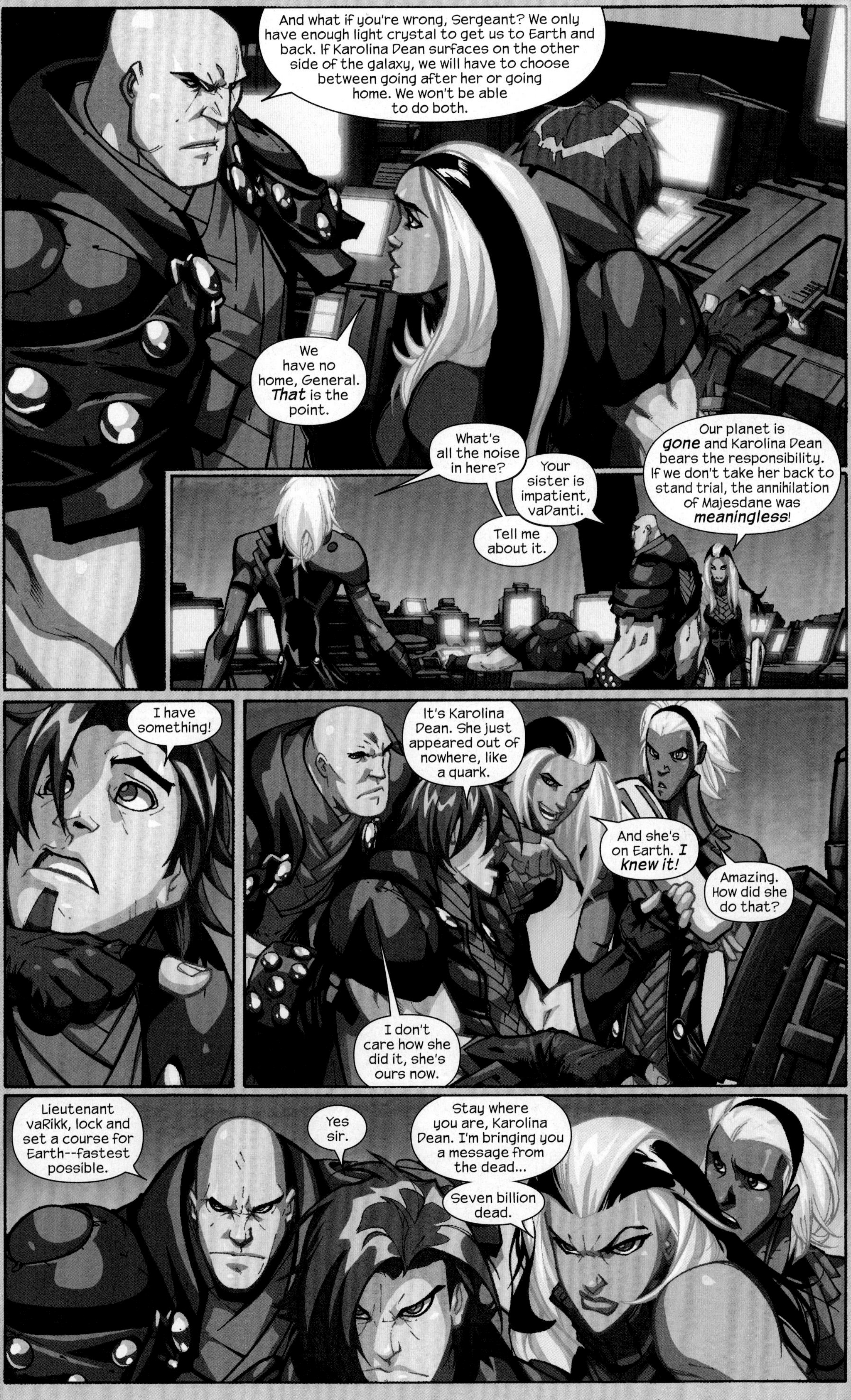
And what if you're wrong, Sergeant? We only have enough light crystal to get us to Earth and back. If Karolina Dean surfaces on the other side of the galaxy, we will have to choose between going after her or going home. We won't be able to do both.
We have no home, General. *That* is the point.
What's all the noise in here?
Your sister is impatient, vaDanti.
Tell me about it.
Our planet is *gone* and Karolina Dean bears the responsibility. If we don't take her back to stand trial, the annihilation of Majesdane was *meaningless*!
I have something!
It's Karolina Dean. She just appeared out of nowhere, like a quark.
And she's on Earth. *I knew it!*
Amazing. How did she do that?
I don't care how she did it, she's ours now.
Lieutenant vaRikk, lock and set a course for Earth--fastest possible.
Yes sir.
Stay where you are, Karolina Dean. I'm bringing you a message from the dead...
Seven billion dead.

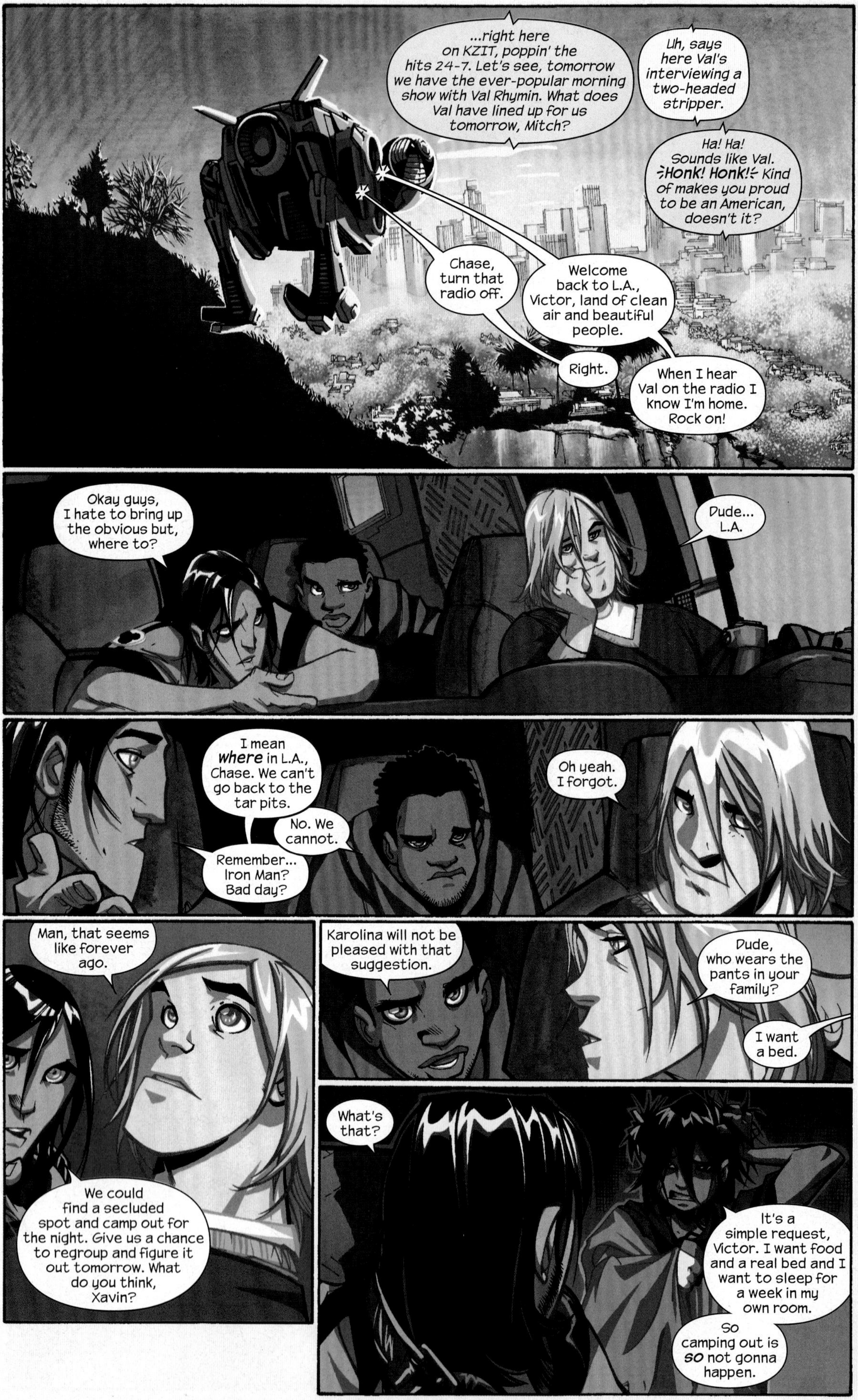
...right here on KZIT, poppin' the hits 24-7. Let's see, tomorrow we have the ever-popular morning show with Val Rhymin. What does Val have lined up for us tomorrow, Mitch?
Uh, says here Val's interviewing a two-headed stripper.
Ha! Ha! Sounds like Val. *Honk! Honk!* Kind of makes you proud to be an American, doesn't it?
Chase, turn that radio off.
Welcome back to L.A., Victor, land of clean air and beautiful people.
Right.
When I hear Val on the radio I know I'm home. Rock on!
Okay guys, I hate to bring up the obvious but, where to?
Dude... L.A.
I mean ***where*** in L.A., Chase. We can't go back to the tar pits.
Remember... Iron Man? Bad day?
No. We cannot.
Oh yeah. I forgot.
Man, that seems like forever ago.
We could find a secluded spot and camp out for the night. Give us a chance to regroup and figure it out tomorrow. What do you think, Xavin?
Karolina will not be pleased with that suggestion.
Dude, who wears the pants in your family?
I want a bed.
What's that?
It's a simple request, Victor. I want food and a real bed and I want to sleep for a week in my own room.
So camping out is ***SO*** not gonna happen.

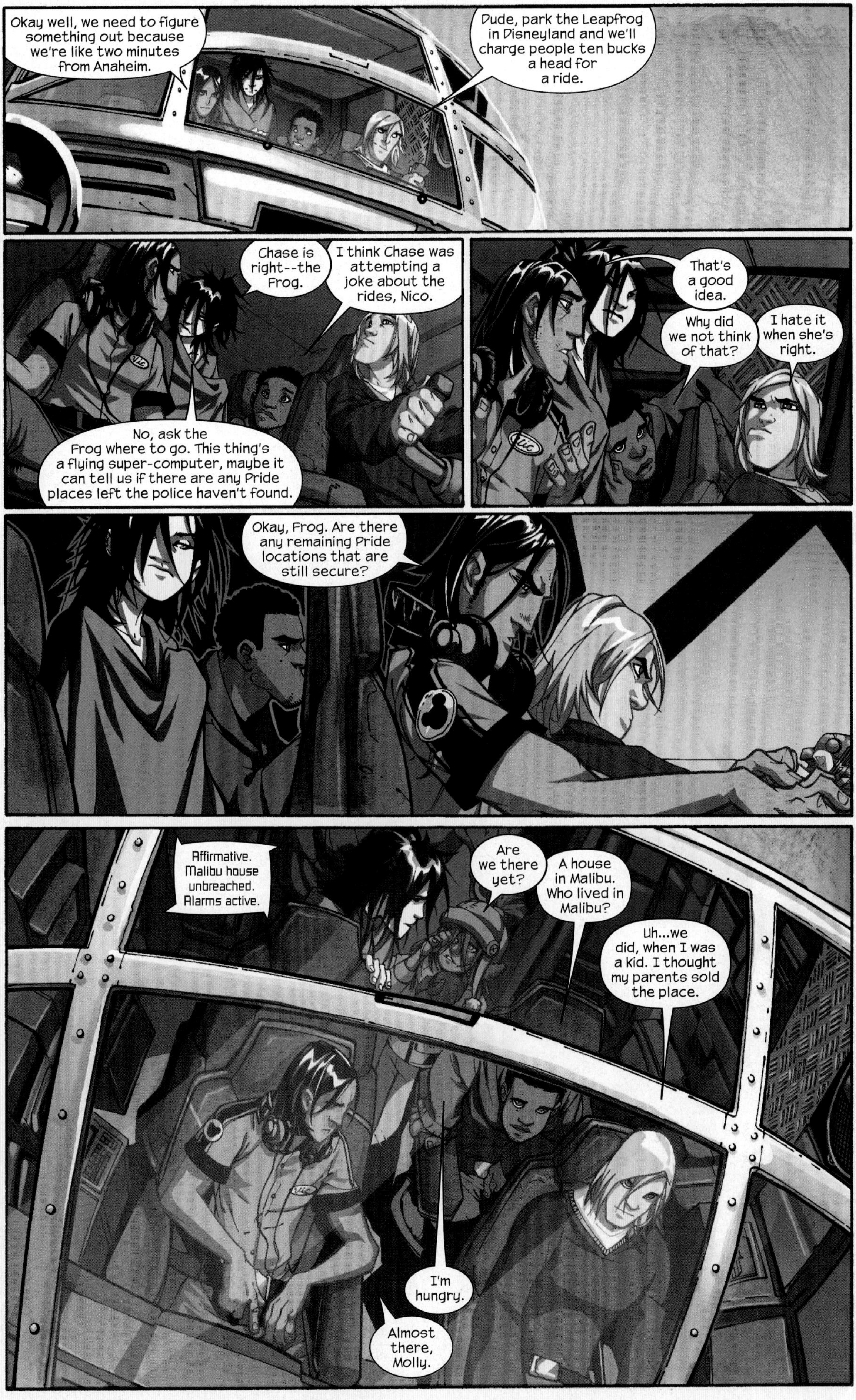
Okay well, we need to figure something out because we're like two minutes from Anaheim.
Dude, park the Leapfrog in Disneyland and we'll charge people ten bucks a head for a ride.
Chase is right--the Frog.
I think Chase was attempting a joke about the rides, Nico.
No, ask the Frog where to go. This thing's a flying super-computer, maybe it can tell us if there are any Pride places left the police haven't found.
That's a good idea.
Why did we not think of that?
I hate it when she's right.
Okay, Frog. Are there any remaining Pride locations that are still secure?
Affirmative. Malibu house unbreached. Alarms active.
Are we there yet?
A house in Malibu. Who lived in Malibu?
Uh...we did, when I was a kid. I thought my parents sold the place.
I'm hungry.
Almost there, Molly.

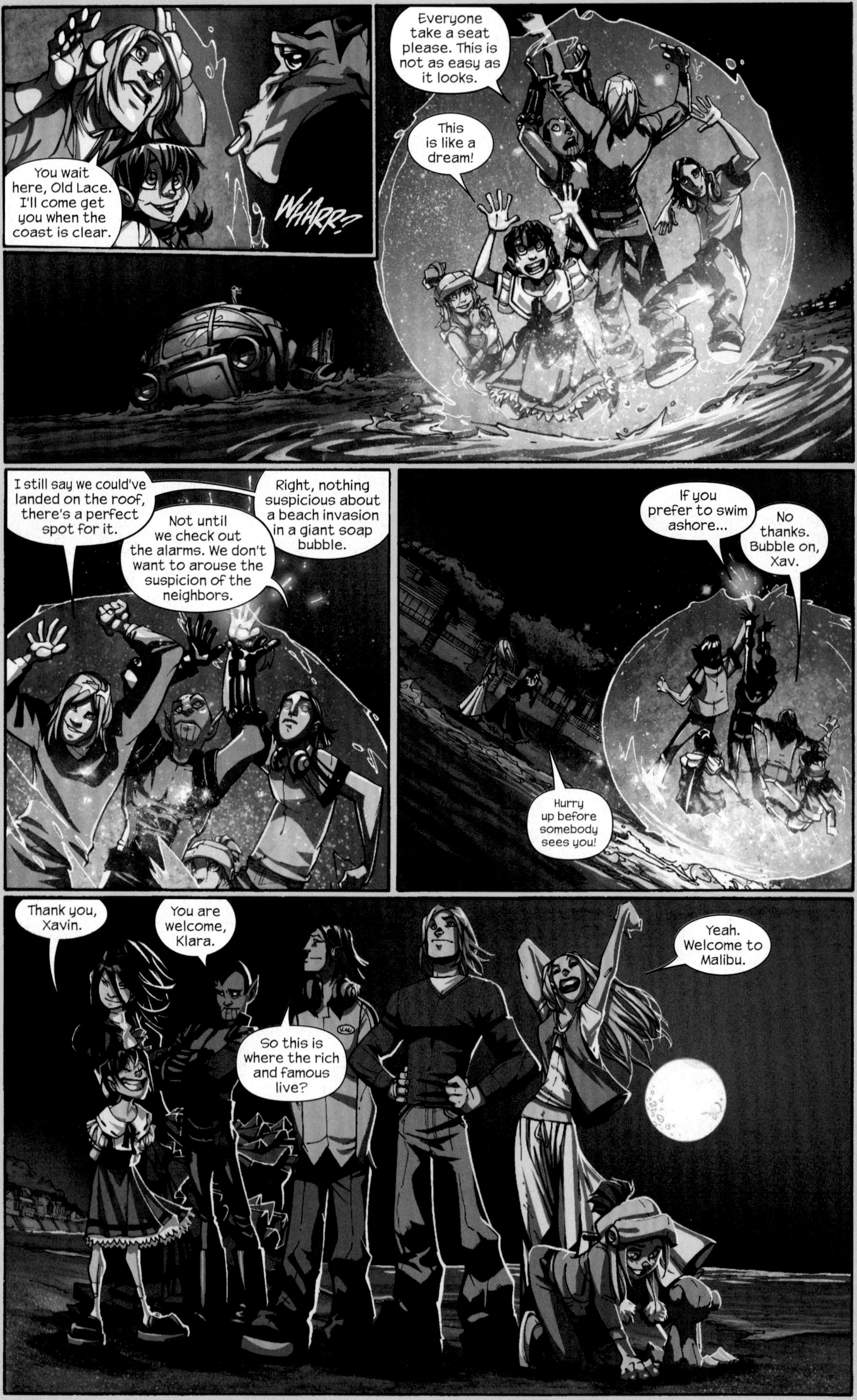

You wait here, Old Lace. I'll come get you when the coast is clear.
WHARR?
Everyone take a seat please. This is not as easy as it looks.
This is like a dream!
I still say we could've landed on the roof, there's a perfect spot for it.
Not until we check out the alarms. We don't want to arouse the suspicion of the neighbors.
Right, nothing suspicious about a beach invasion in a giant soap bubble.
If you prefer to swim ashore...
No thanks. Bubble on, Xav.
Hurry up before somebody sees you!
Thank you, Xavin.
You are welcome, Klara.
So this is where the rich and famous live?
Yeah. Welcome to Malibu.

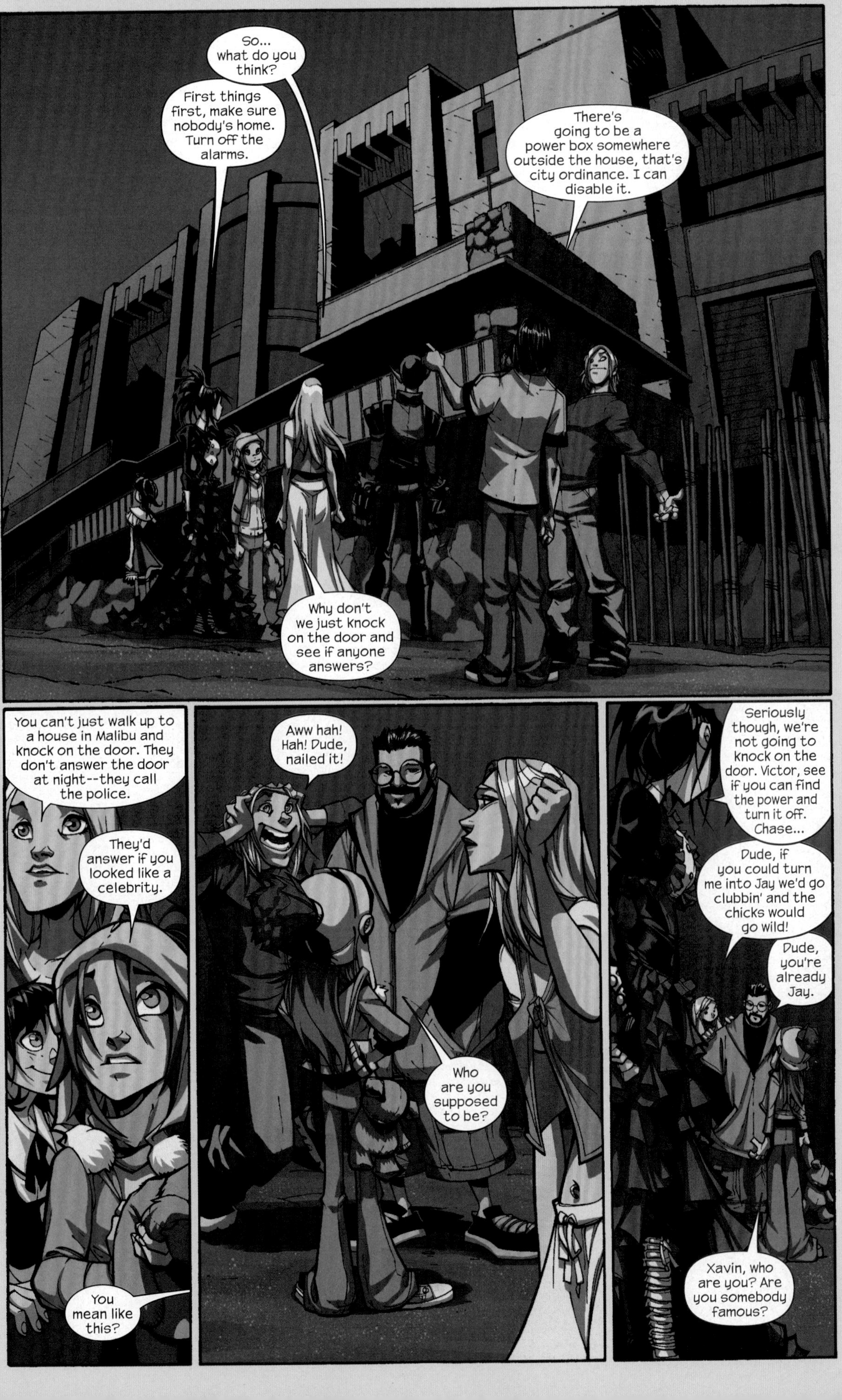
So... what do you think?
First things first, make sure nobody's home. Turn off the alarms.
There's going to be a power box somewhere outside the house, that's city ordinance. I can disable it.
Why don't we just knock on the door and see if anyone answers?
You can't just walk up to a house in Malibu and knock on the door. They don't answer the door at night--they call the police.
They'd answer if you looked like a celebrity.
You mean like this?
Aww hah! Hah! Dude, nailed it!
Who are you supposed to be?
Seriously though, we're not going to knock on the door. Victor, see if you can find the power and turn it off. Chase...
Dude, if you could turn me into Jay we'd go clubbin' and the chicks would go wild!
Dude, you're already Jay.
Xavin, who are you? Are you somebody famous?

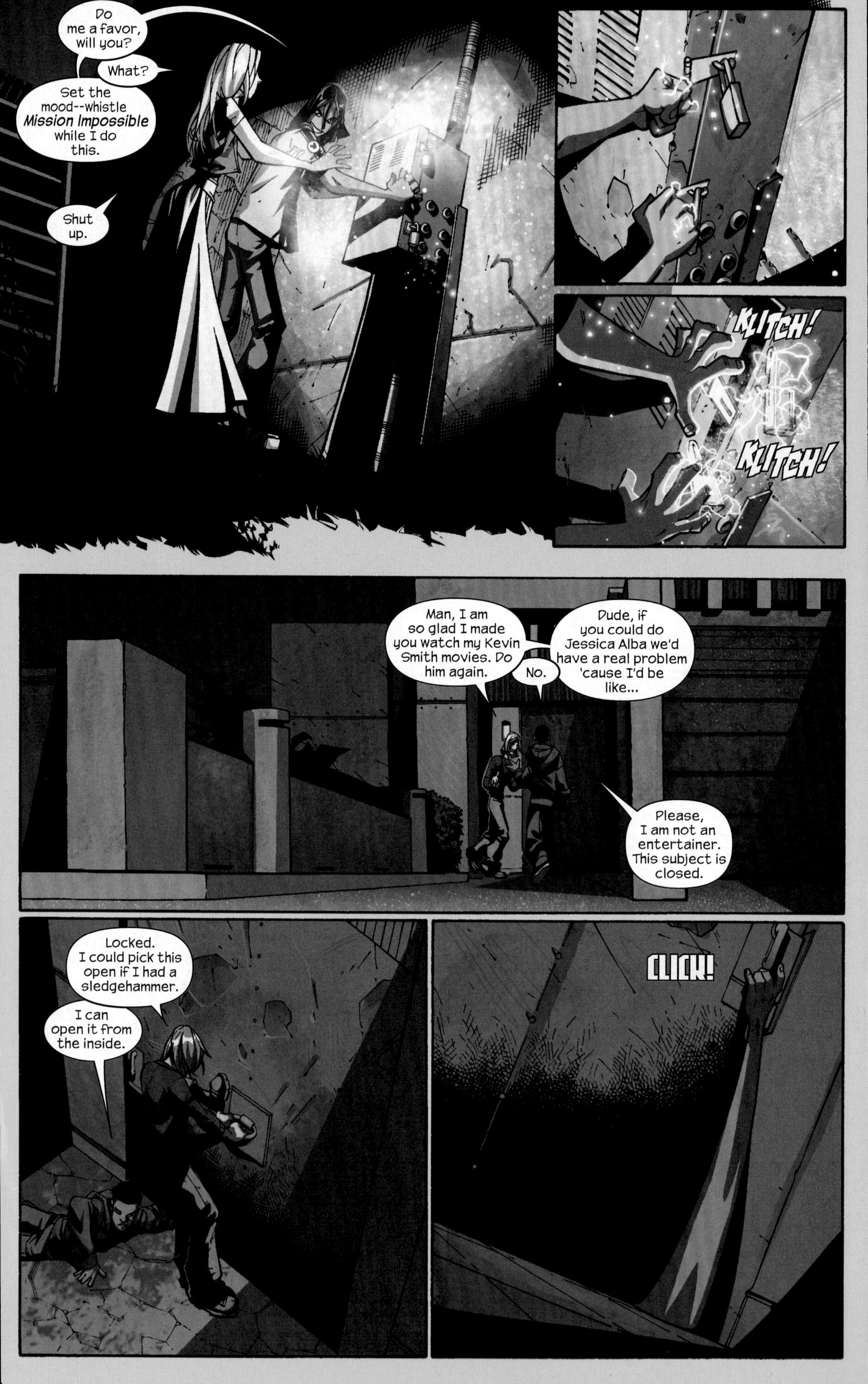
Do me a favor, will you?
What?
Set the mood--whistle *Mission Impossible* while I do this.
Shut up.
KLITCH!
KLITCH!
Man, I am so glad I made you watch my Kevin Smith movies. Do him again.
No.
Dude, if you could do Jessica Alba we'd have a real problem 'cause I'd be like...
Please, I am not an entertainer. This subject is closed.
Locked. I could pick this open if I had a sledgehammer.
I can open it from the inside.
CLICK!

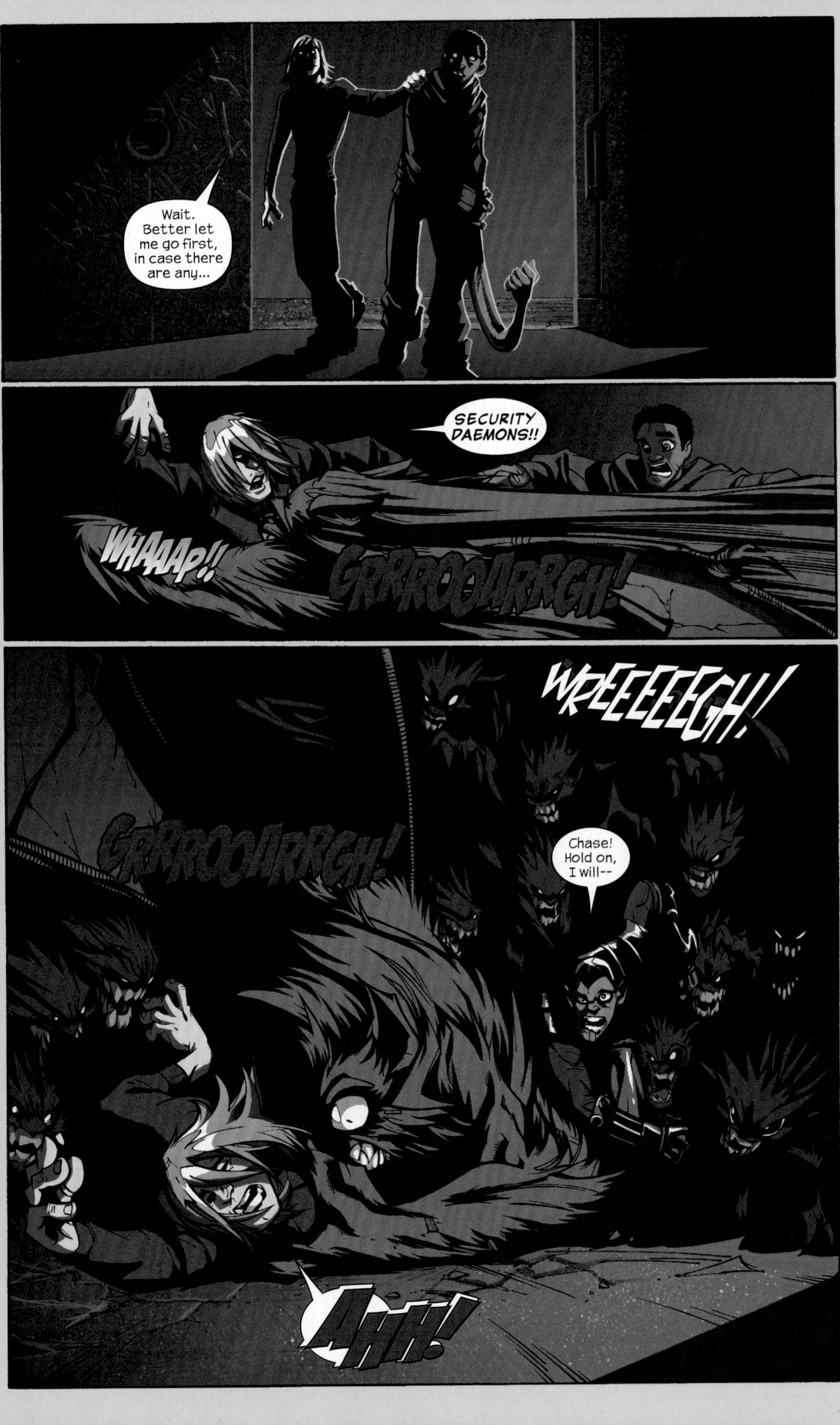
Wait. Better let me go first, in case there are any...
SECURITY DAEMONS!!
WHAAAP!!
GRRROOARRRGH!
WREEEEEEGH!
GRRROOARRRGH!
Chase! Hold on, I will--
AHH!

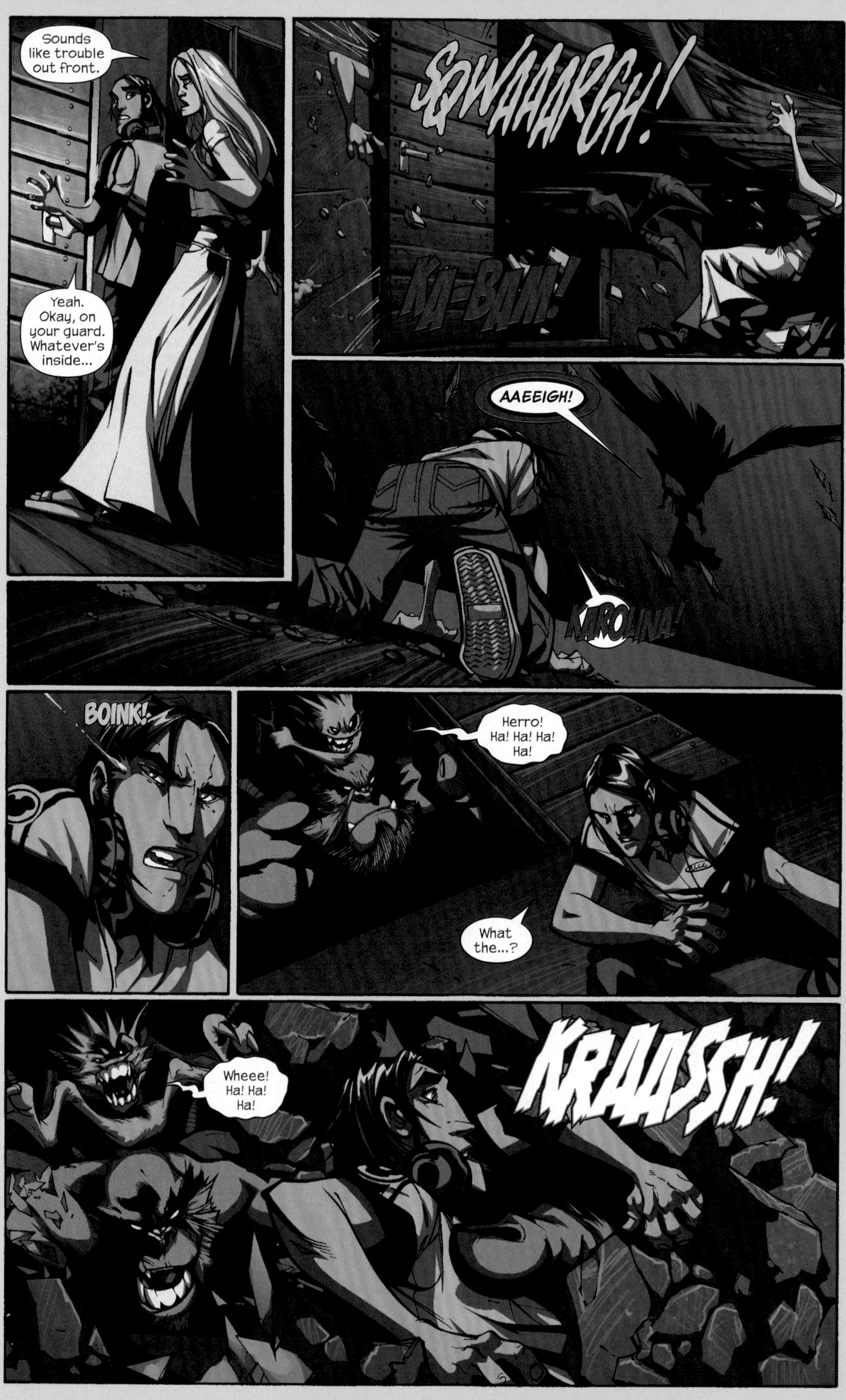
Sounds like trouble out front.
Yeah. Okay, on your guard. Whatever's inside...
SQWAAARGH!
KA-BAM!
AAEEIGH!
KAROLINA!
BOINK!
Herro! Ha! Ha! Ha! Ha!
What the...?
Wheee! Ha! Ha! Ha!
KRAASH!

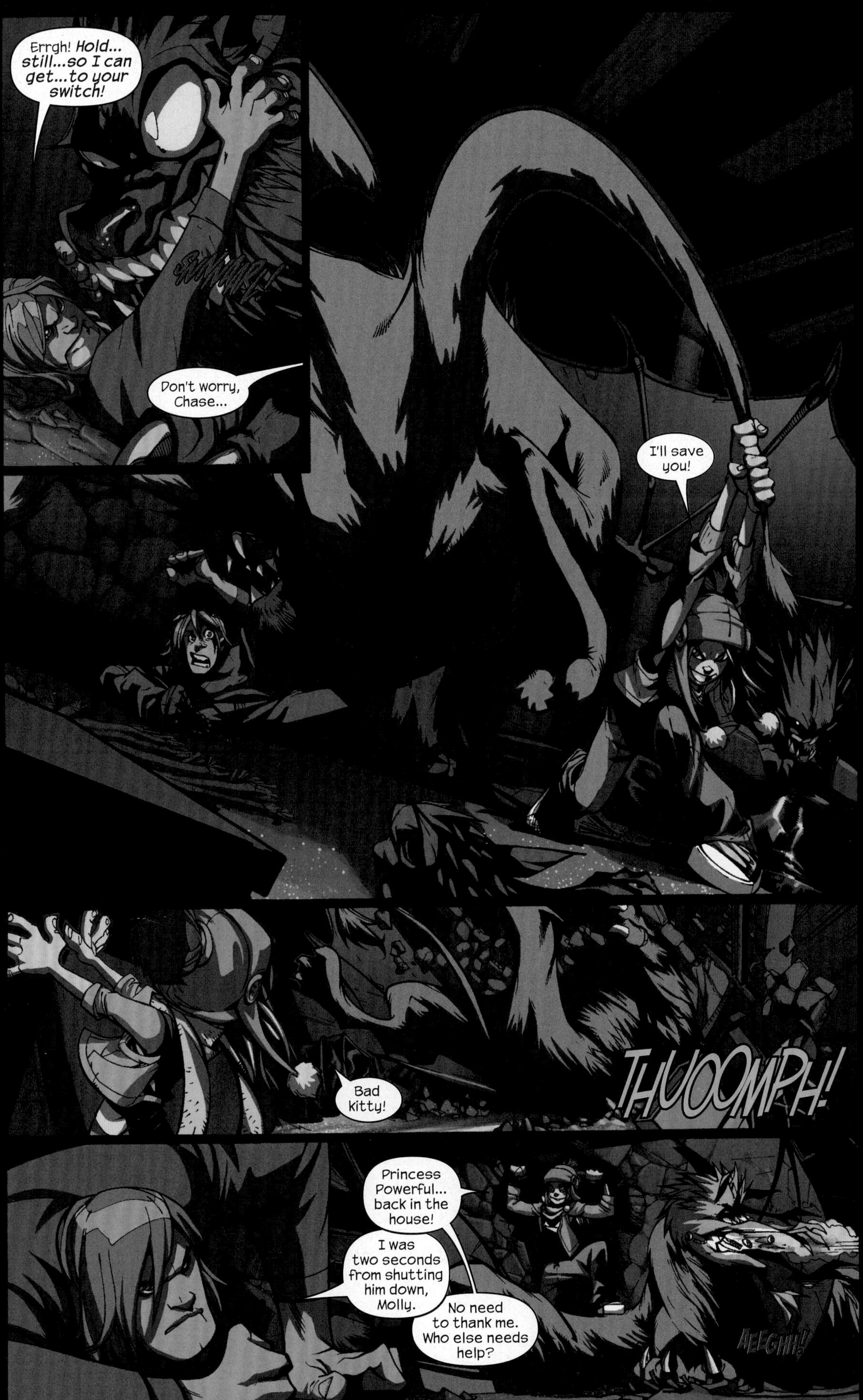
Errgh! Hold... still...so I can get...to your switch!
Don't worry, Chase...
I'll save you!
Bad kitty!
THUOOMPH!
Princess Powerful... back in the house!
I was two seconds from shutting him down, Molly.
No need to thank me. Who else needs help?
AEEGHH!

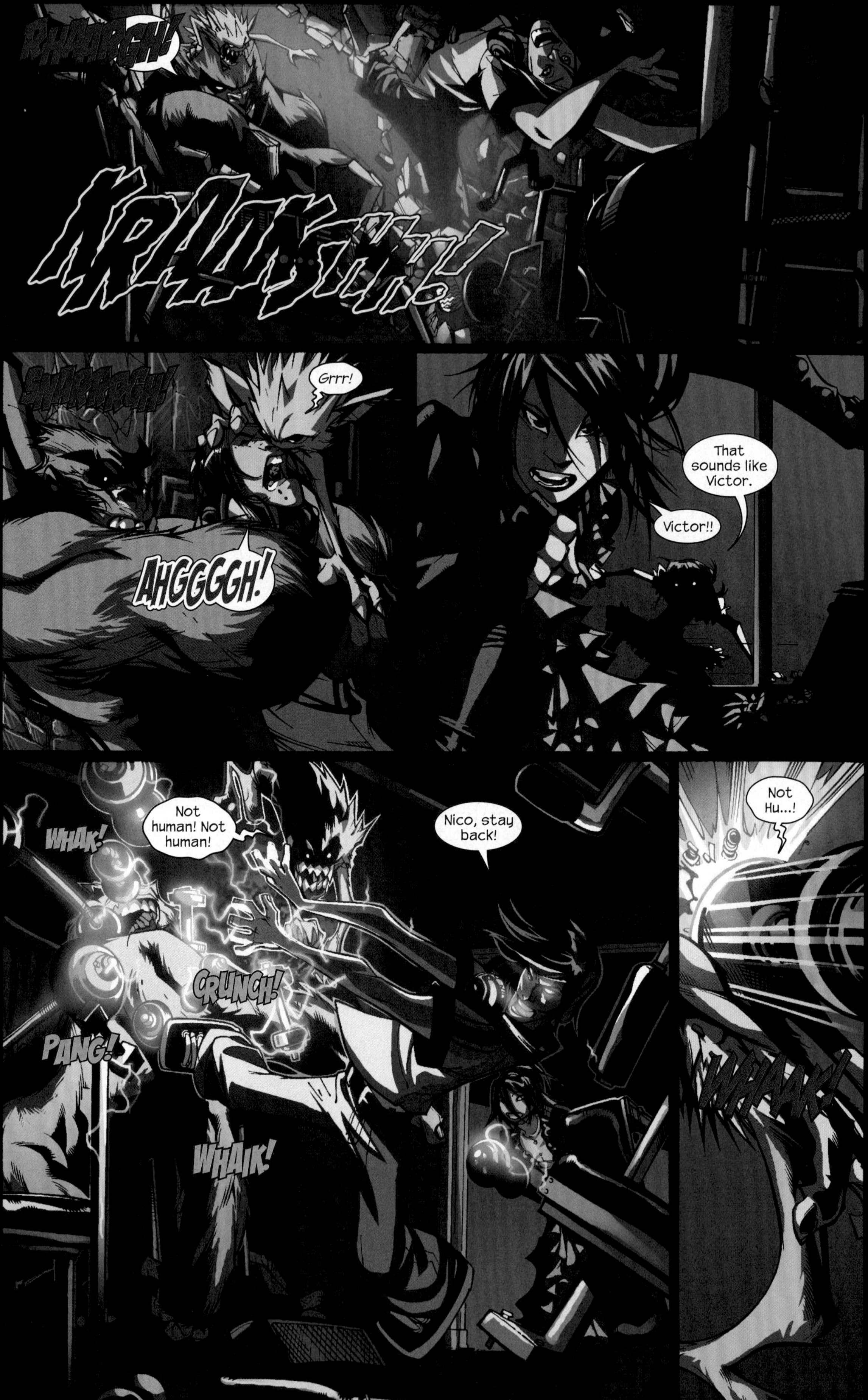
RHAAARGH!
KRAASHHH!
Grrr!
AHGGGGH!
Victor!!
That sounds like Victor.
WHAK!
Not human! Not human!
Nico, stay back!
CRUNCH!
PANG!
WHAIK!
Not Hu...!
WHAAK!

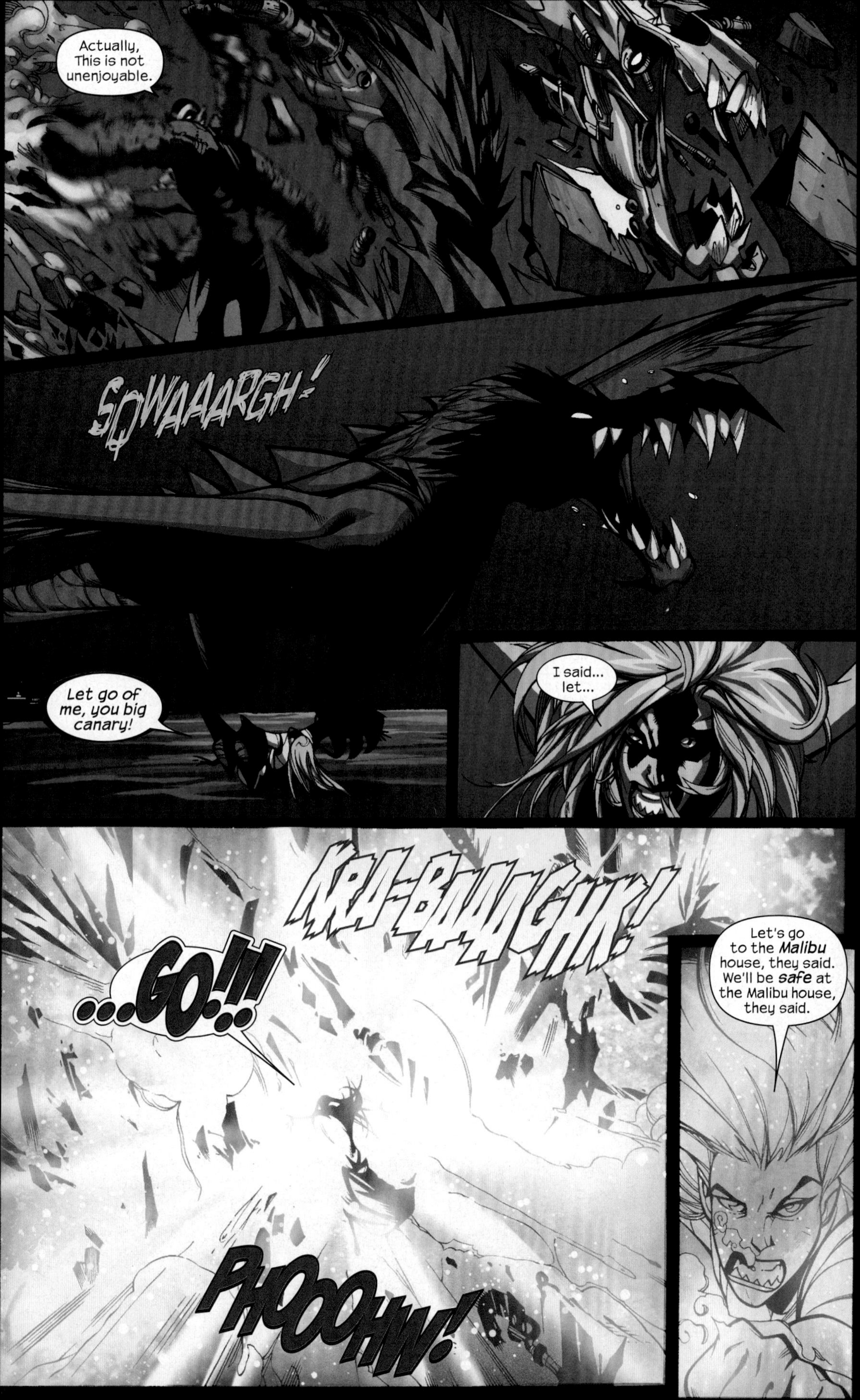
Actually, This is not unenjoyable.
SQWAAARGH!
Let go of me, you big canary!
I said... let...
KRA-BAUGHK!
...GO!!!
Let's go to the *Malibu* house, they said. We'll be *safe* at the Malibu house, they said.
PHOOOHW!

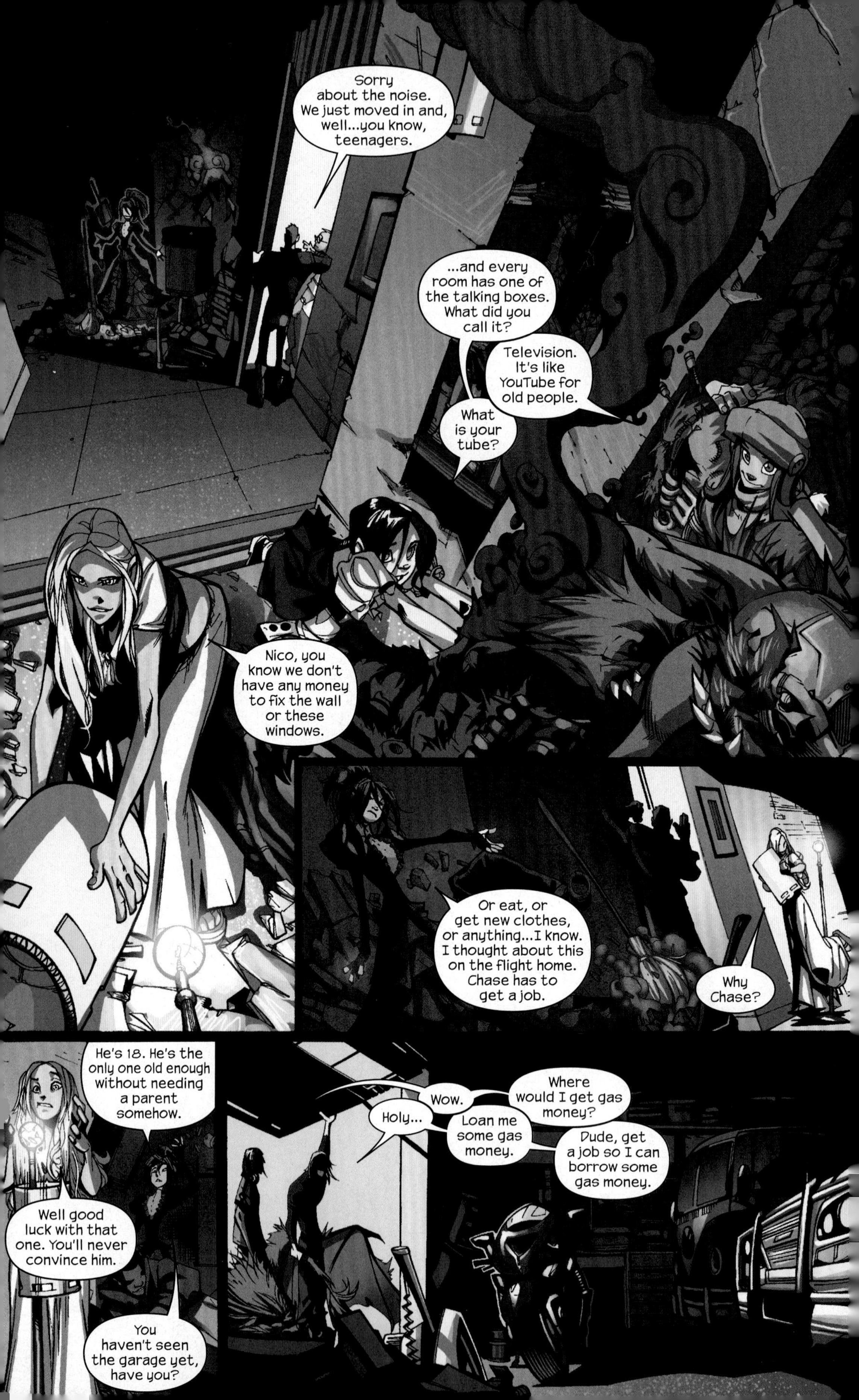
Sorry about the noise. We just moved in and, well...you know, teenagers.
...and every room has one of the talking boxes. What did you call it?
Television. It's like YouTube for old people.
What is your tube?
Nico, you know we don't have any money to fix the wall or these windows.
Or eat, or get new clothes, or anything...I know. I thought about this on the flight home. Chase has to get a job.
Why Chase?
He's 18. He's the only one old enough without needing a parent somehow.
Well good luck with that one. You'll never convince him.
You haven't seen the garage yet, have you?
Wow.
Holy...
Where would I get gas money?
Loan me some gas money.
Dude, get a job so I can borrow some gas money.

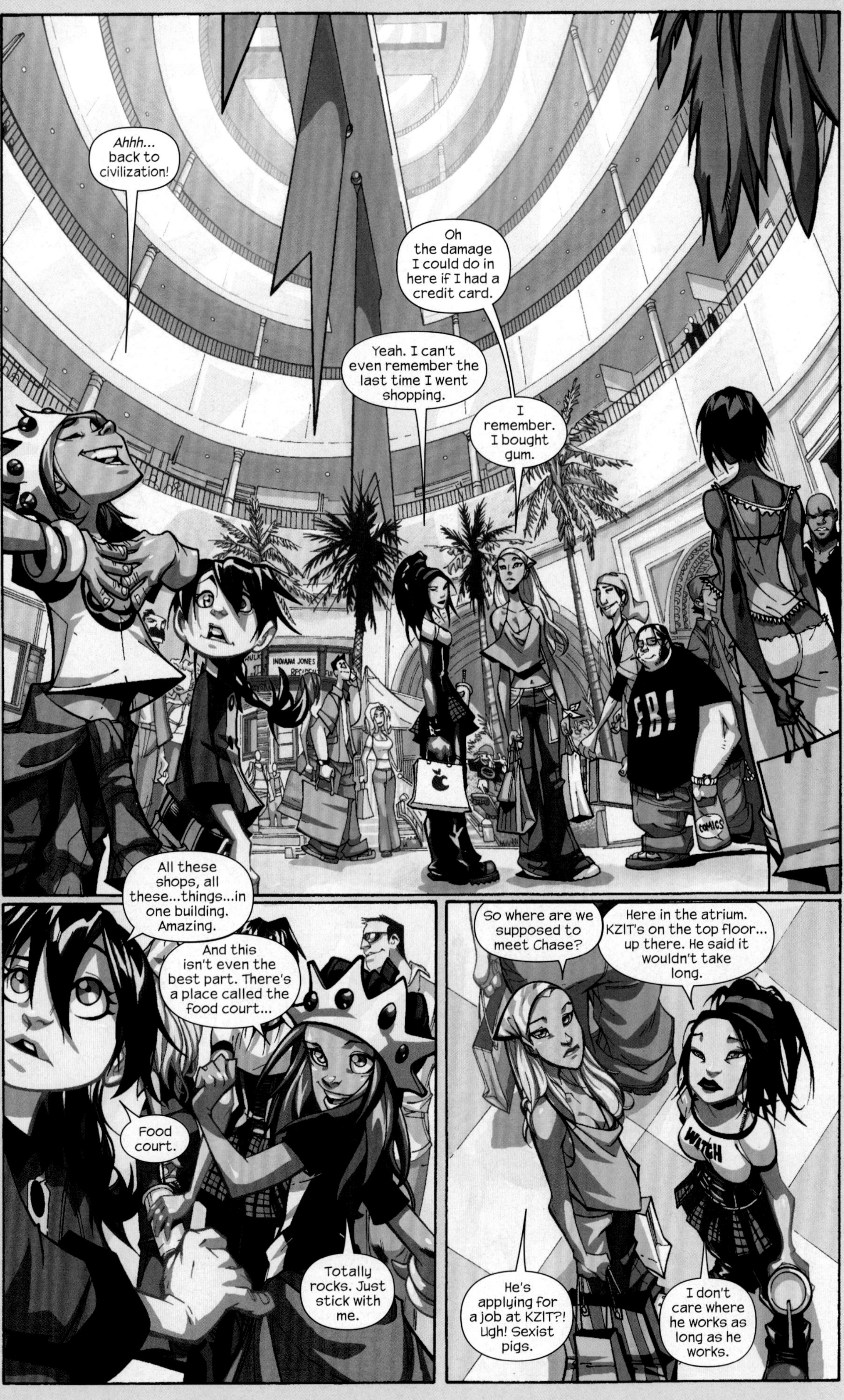
Ahhh... back to civilization!
Oh the damage I could do in here if I had a credit card.
Yeah. I can't even remember the last time I went shopping.
I remember. I bought gum.
INDIANA JONES
FBI
COMICS
All these shops, all these...things...in one building. Amazing.
And this isn't even the best part. There's a place called the food court...
Food court.
Totally rocks. Just stick with me.
So where are we supposed to meet Chase?
Here in the atrium. KZIT's on the top floor... up there. He said it wouldn't take long.
WITCH
He's applying for a job at KZIT?! Ugh! Sexist pigs.
I don't care where he works as long as he works.

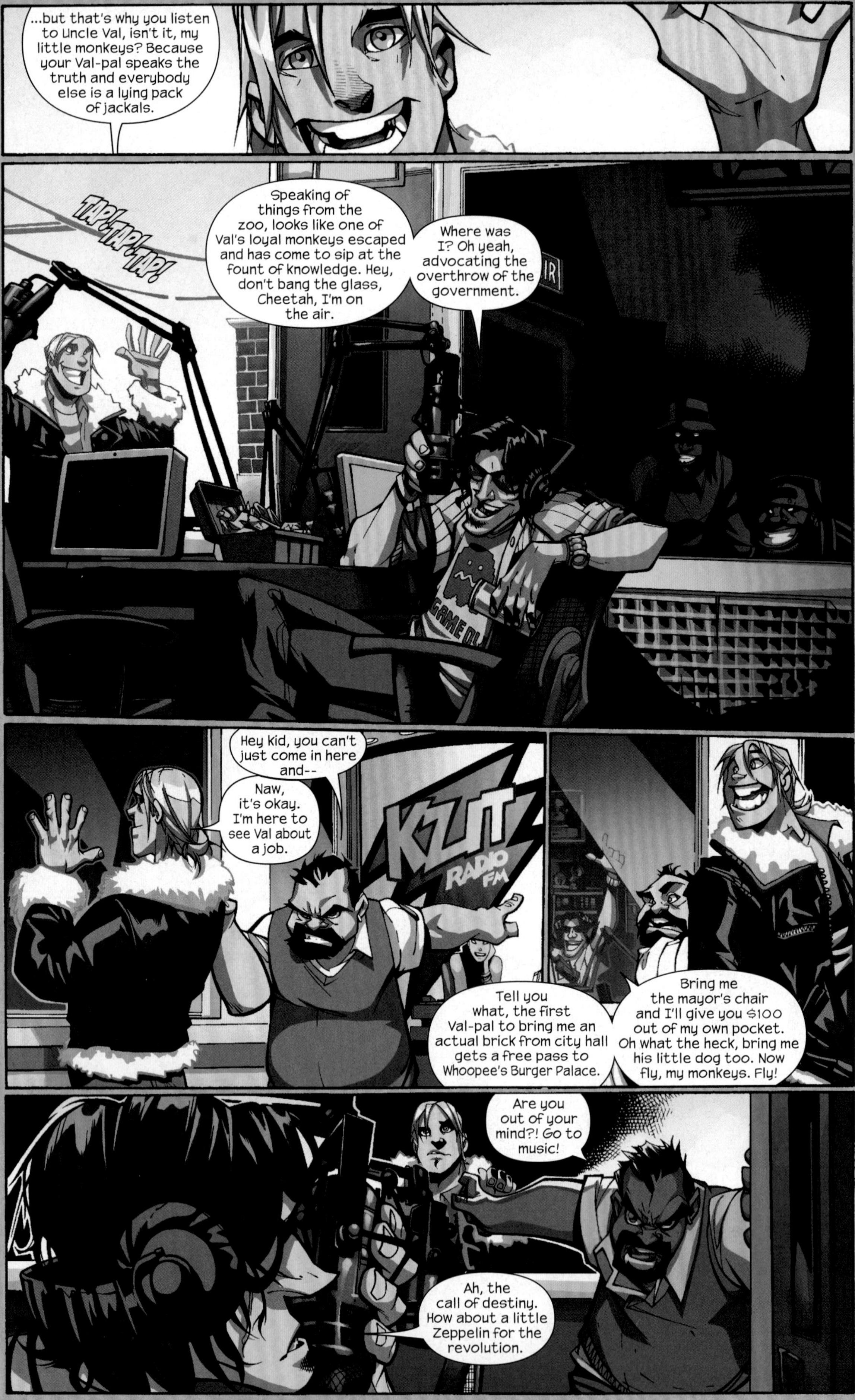
...but that's why you listen to Uncle Val, isn't it, my little monkeys? Because your Val-pal speaks the truth and everybody else is a lying pack of jackals.
TAP! TAP! TAP!
Speaking of things from the zoo, looks like one of Val's loyal monkeys escaped and has come to sip at the fount of knowledge. Hey, don't bang the glass, Cheetah, I'm on the air.
Where was I? Oh yeah, advocating the overthrow of the government.
Hey kid, you can't just come in here and--
Naw, it's okay. I'm here to see Val about a job.
KZIT RADIO FM
Tell you what, the first Val-pal to bring me an actual brick from city hall gets a free pass to Whoopee's Burger Palace.
Bring me the mayor's chair and I'll give you $100 out of my own pocket. Oh what the heck, bring me his little dog too. Now fly, my monkeys. Fly!
Are you out of your mind?! Go to music!
Ah, the call of destiny. How about a little Zeppelin for the revolution.

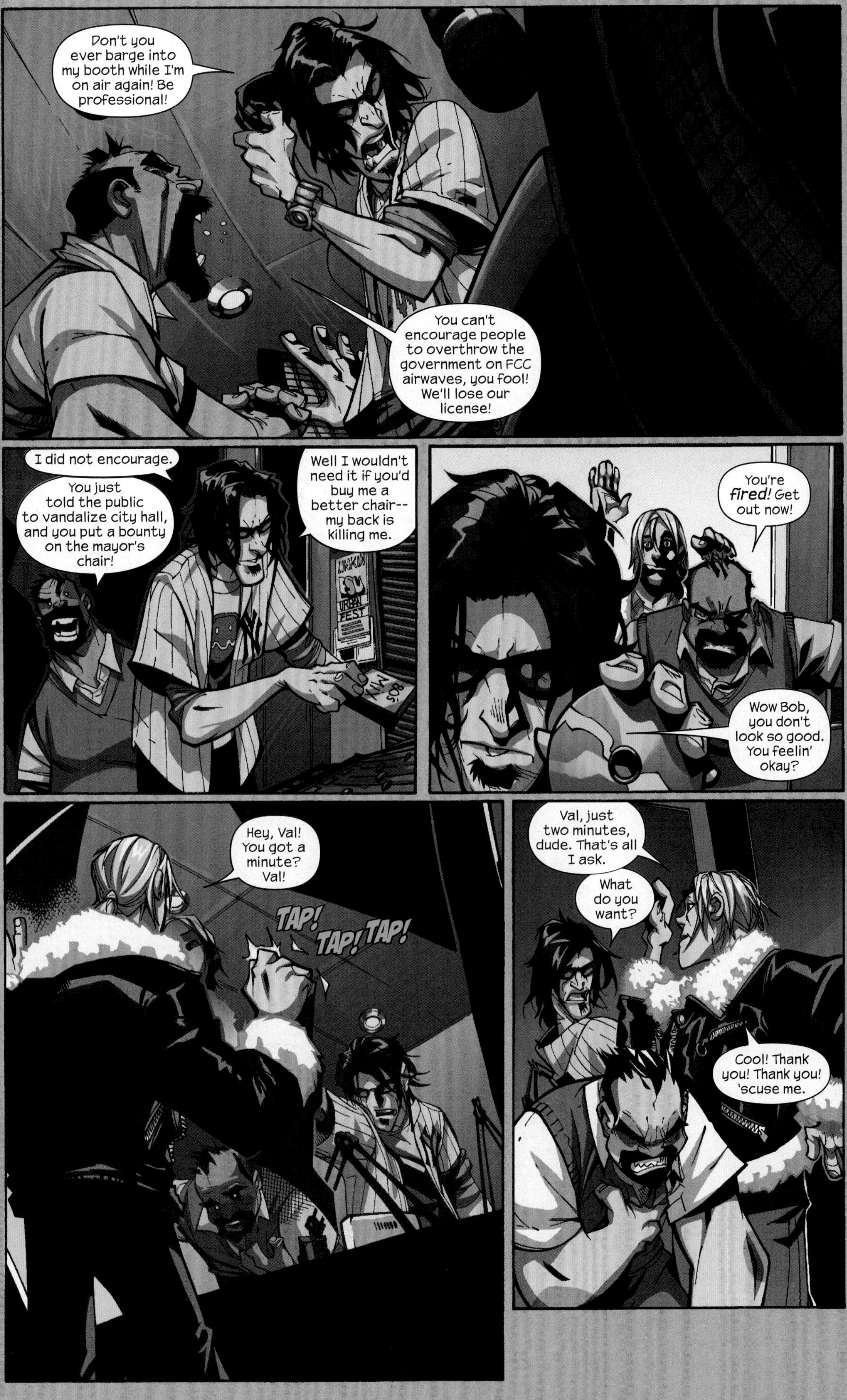

Don't you ever barge into my booth while I'm on air again! Be professional!
You can't encourage people to overthrow the government on FCC airwaves, you fool! We'll lose our license!
I did not encourage.
You just told the public to vandalize city hall, and you put a bounty on the mayor's chair!
Well I wouldn't need it if you'd buy me a better chair--my back is killing me.
URBAN FEST
You're *fired!* Get out now!
Wow Bob, you don't look so good. You feelin' okay?
Hey, Val! You got a minute? Val!
TAP! TAP! TAP!
Val, just two minutes, dude. That's all I ask.
What do you want?
Cool! Thank you! Thank you! 'scuse me.

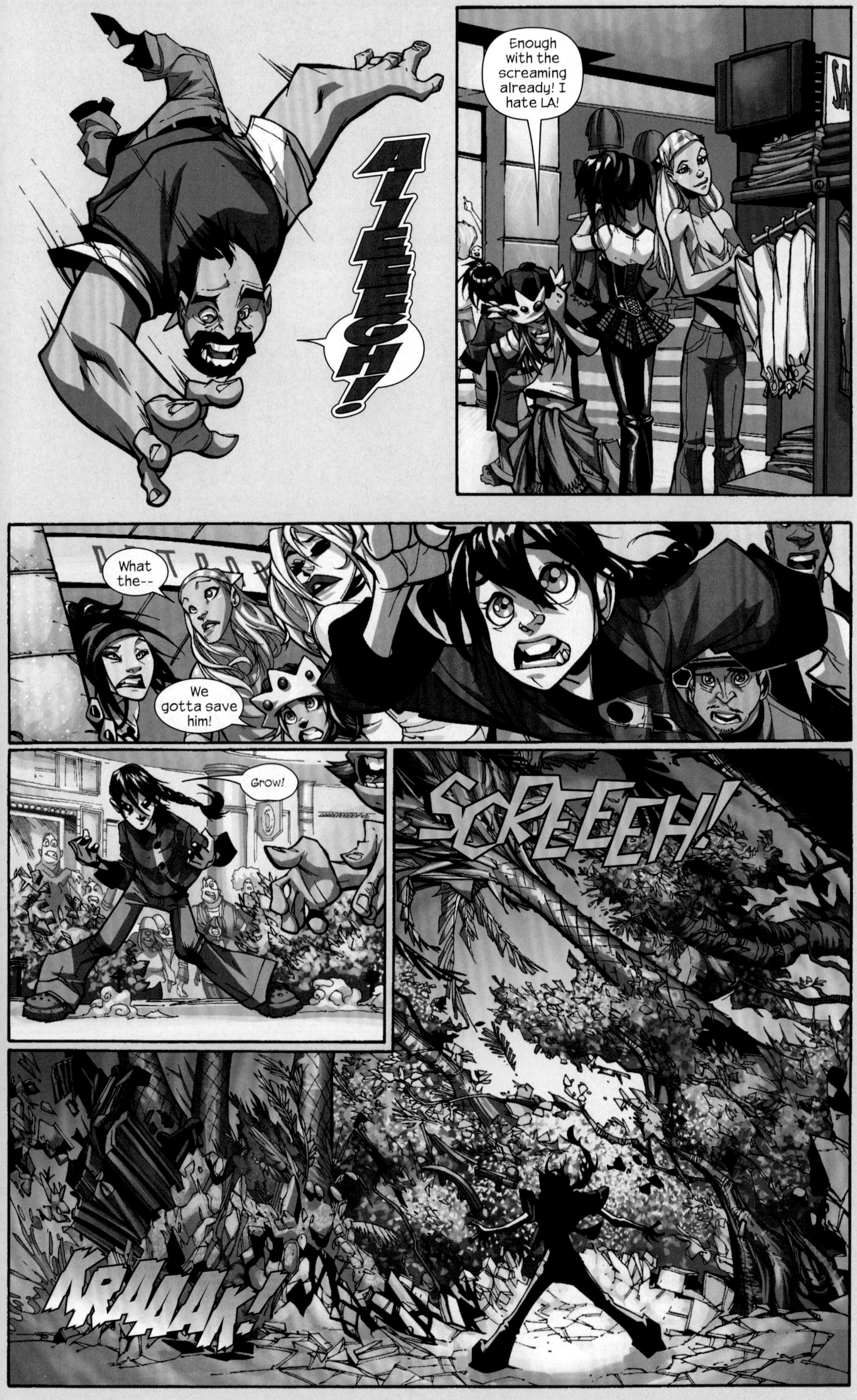
AIIEEECH!
Enough with the screaming already! I hate LA!
What the--
We gotta save him!
Grow!
SCREEEH!
KRAAAK!

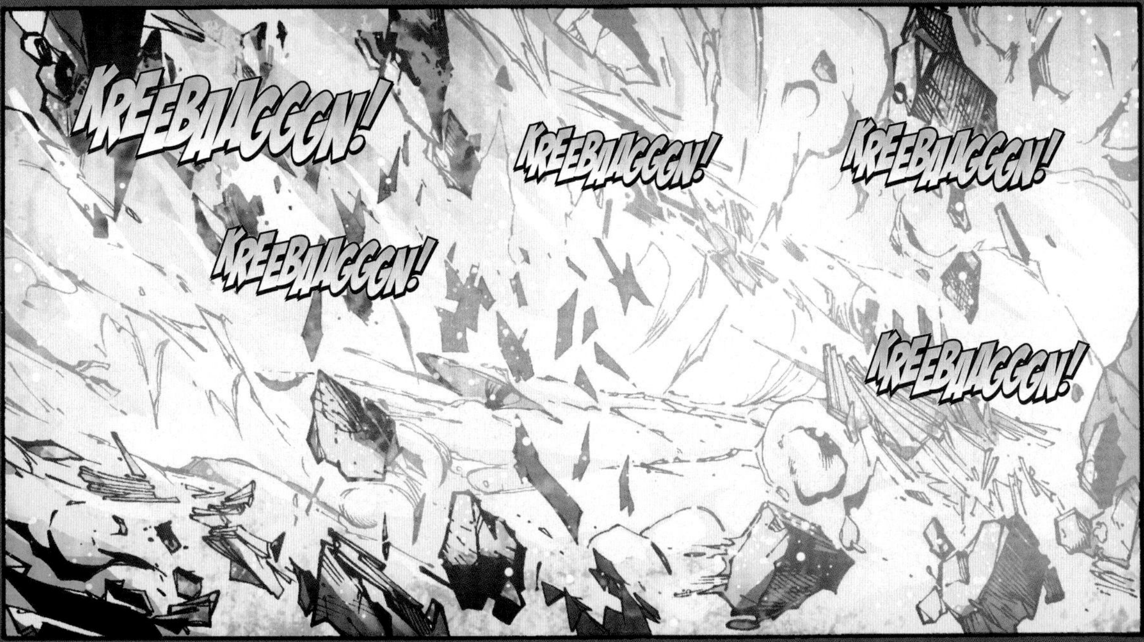
KREEBAAGGGN!
KREEBAAGGGN!
KREEBAAGGGN!
KREEBAAGGGN!
KREEBAAGGGN!

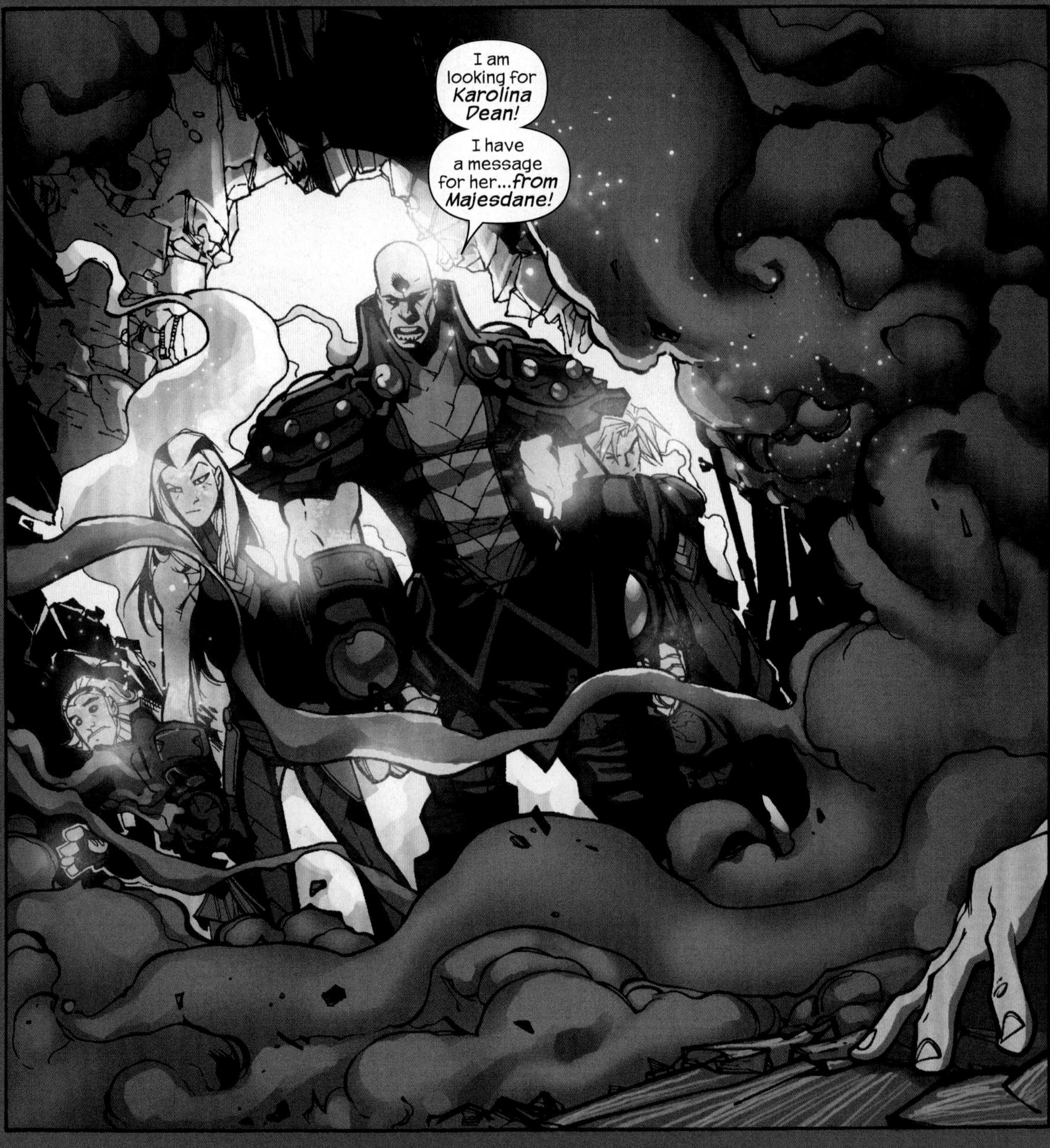
I am looking for *Karolina Dean!*
I have a message for her...*from Majesdane!*

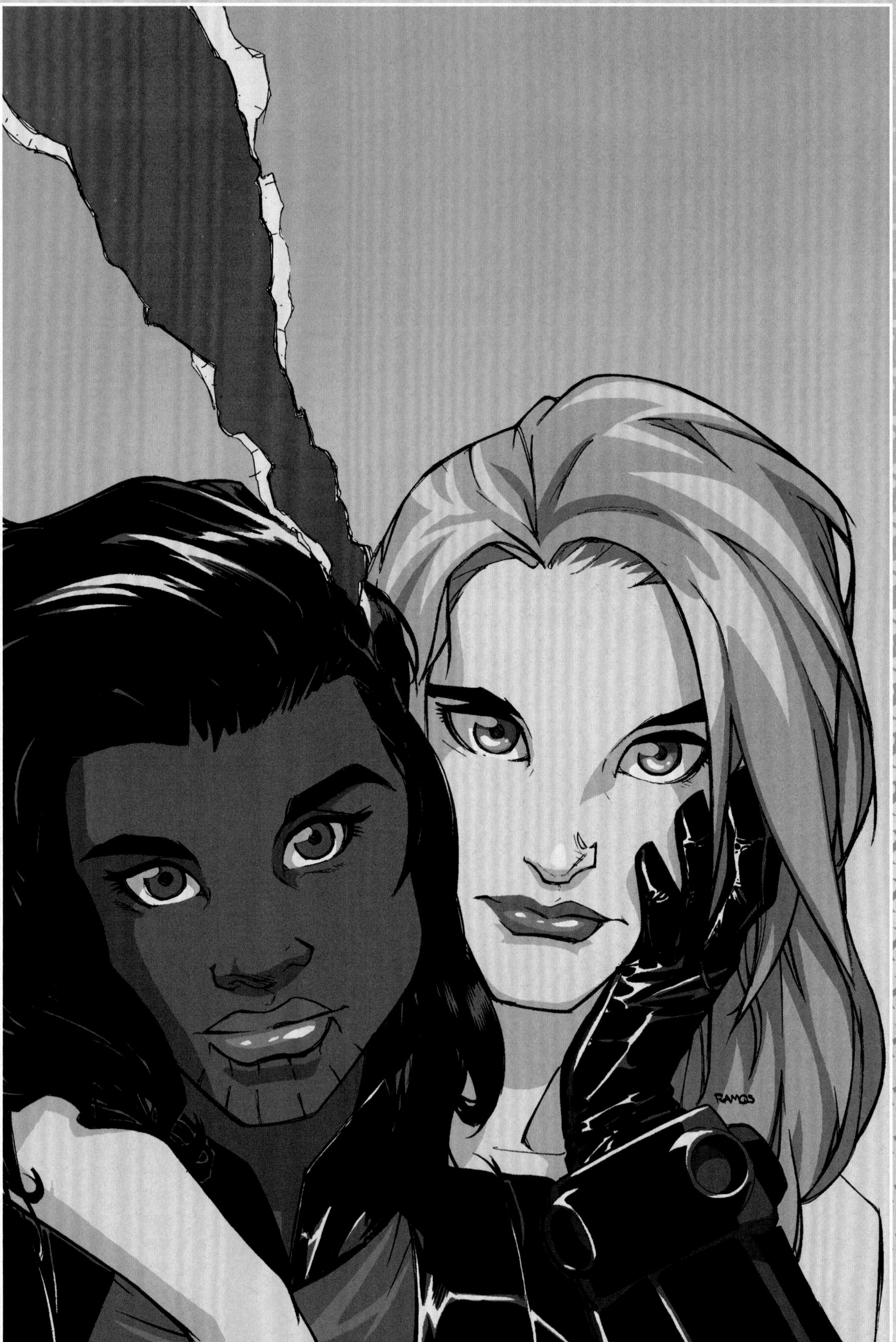
RAMOS

2

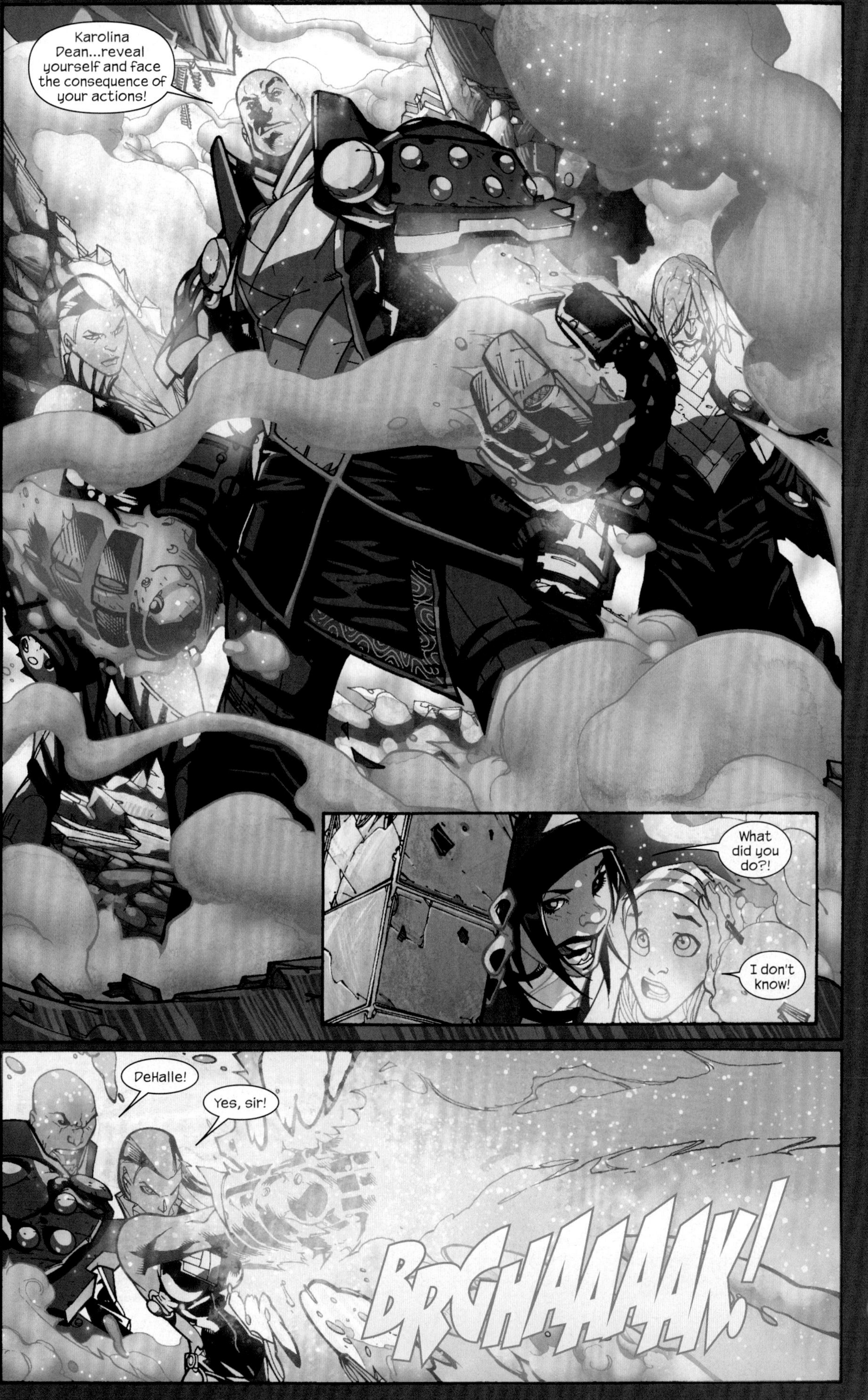
Karolina Dean...reveal yourself and face the consequence of your actions!
What did you do?!
I don't know!
DeHalle!
Yes, sir!
BRGHAAAAK!

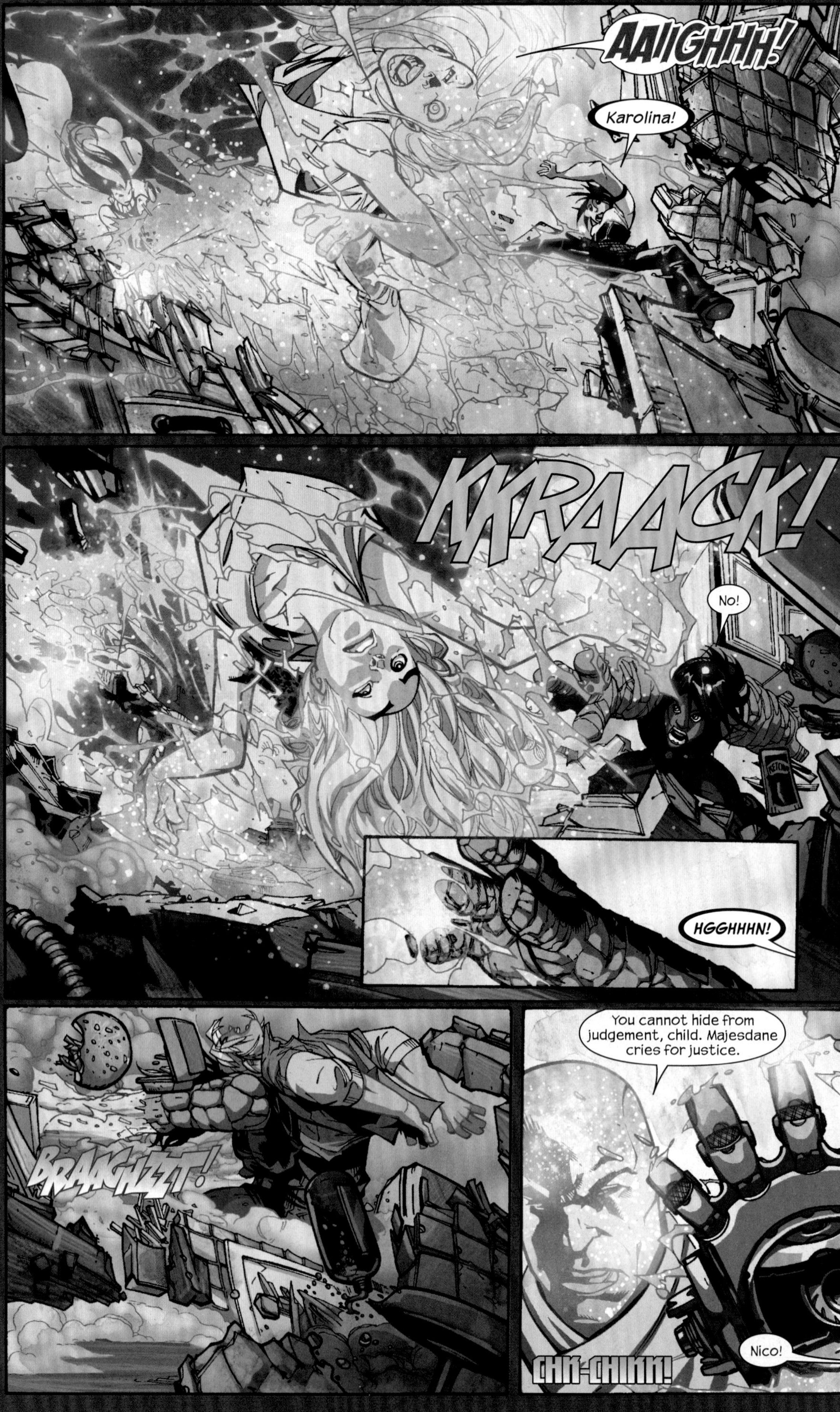
AAIIGHHH!
Karolina!
KKRAACK!
No!
HGGHHHN!
BRAAGHZZT!
You cannot hide from judgement, child. Majesdane cries for justice.
Nico!
CHK-CHINK!

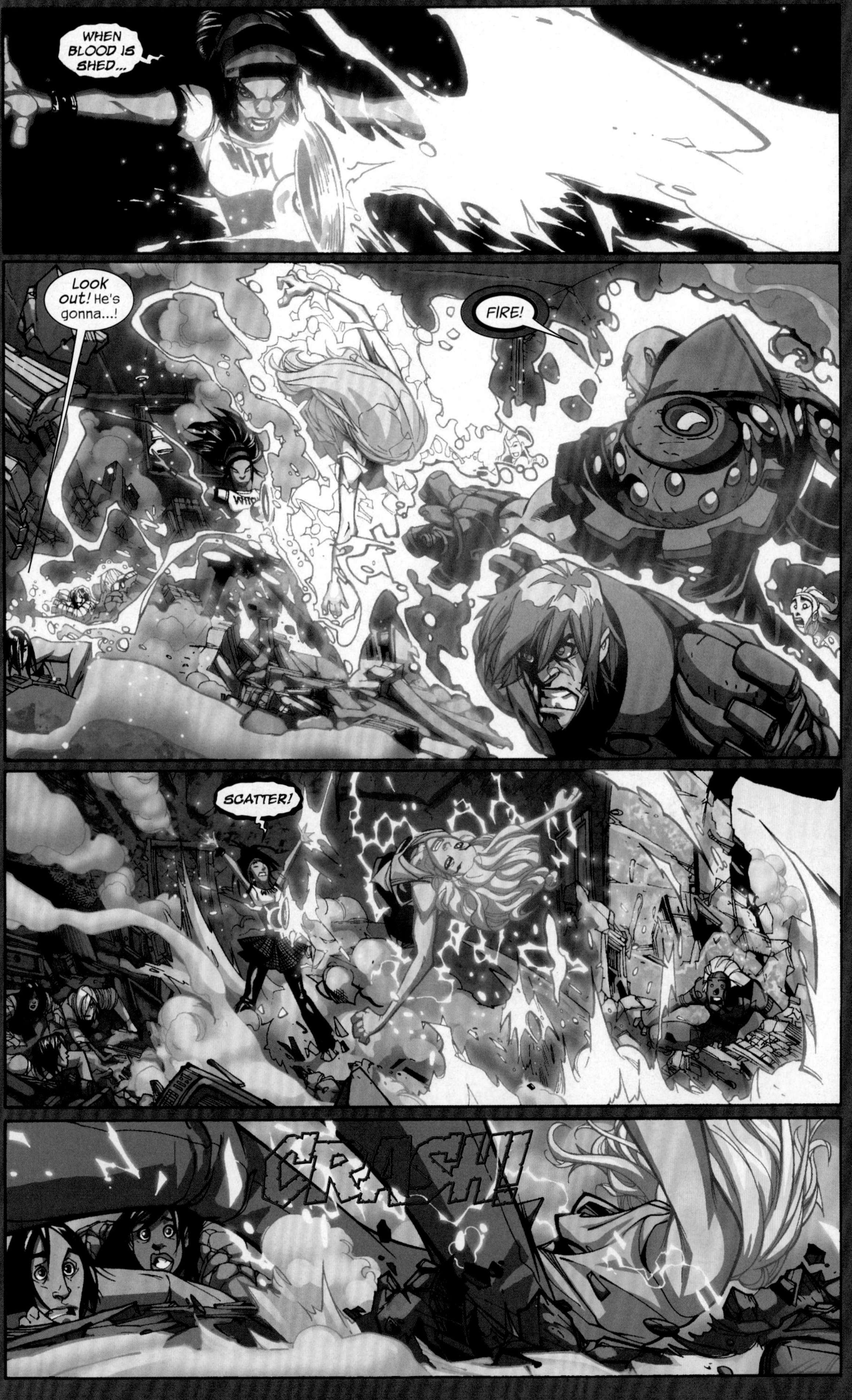

WHEN BLOOD IS SHED...
Look out! He's gonna...!
FIRE!
SCATTER!
CRASH!

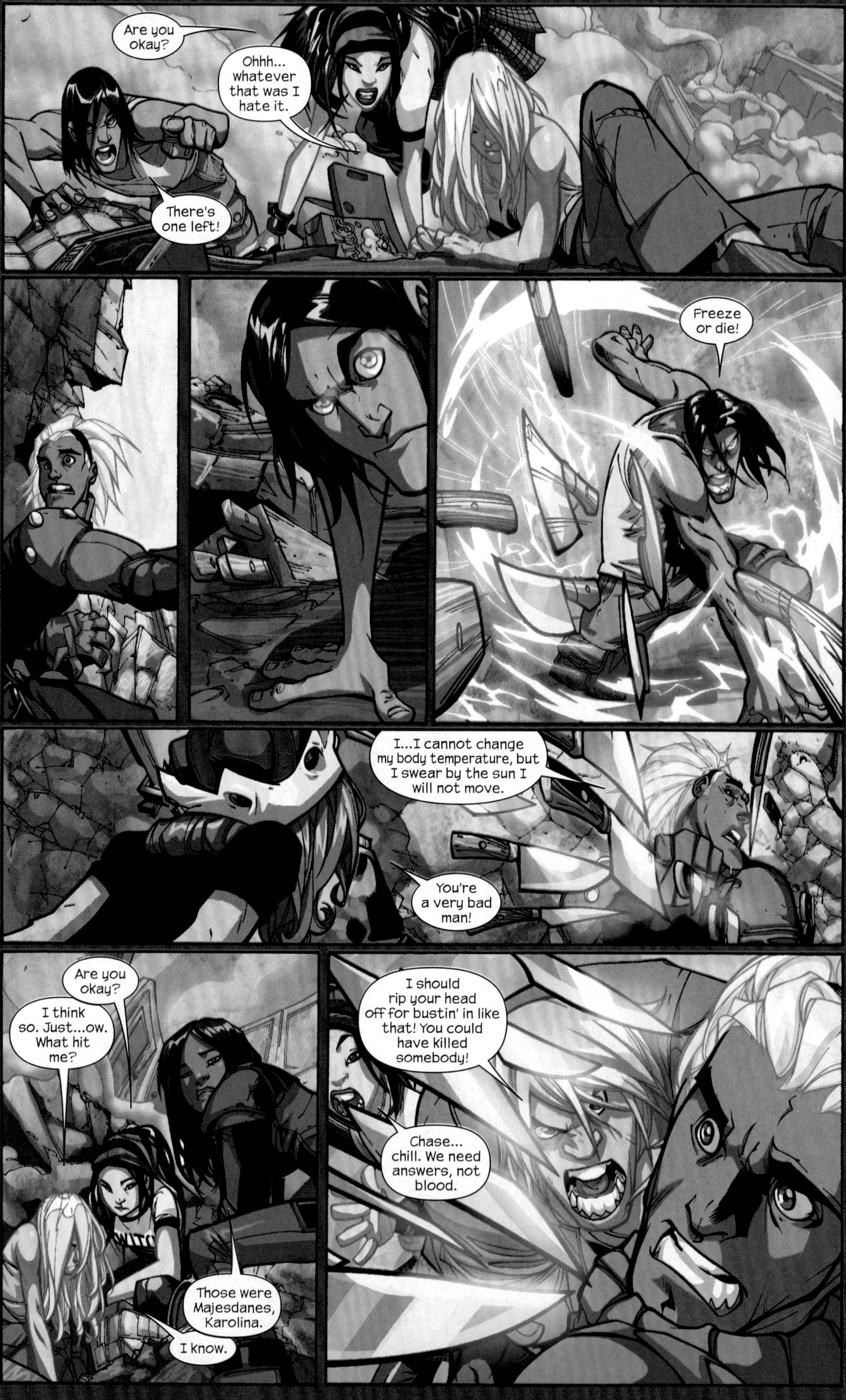
Are you okay?
Ohhh... whatever that was I hate it.
There's one left!
Freeze or die!
I...I cannot change my body temperature, but I swear by the sun I will not move.
You're a very bad man!
Are you okay?
I think so. Just...ow. What hit me?
Those were Majesdanes, Karolina.
I know.
I should rip your head off for bustin' in like that! You could have killed somebody!
Chase... chill. We need answers, not blood.

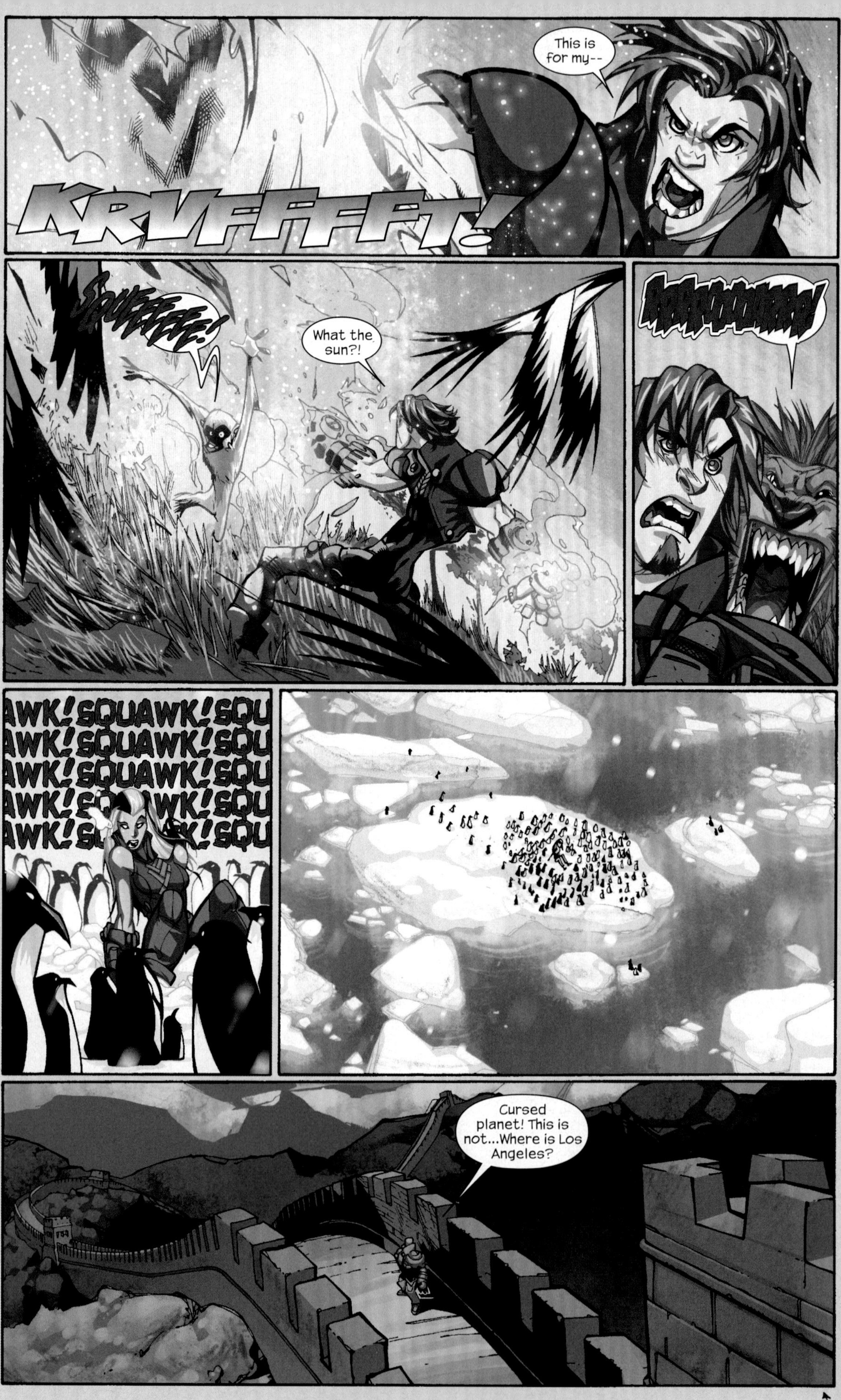
This is for my--
KRVFFFFT!
SQUEEEEEE!
What the sun?!
AWK! SQUAWK! SQU
AWK! SQUAWK! SQU
AWK! SQUAWK! SQU
Cursed planet! This is not...Where is Los Angeles?

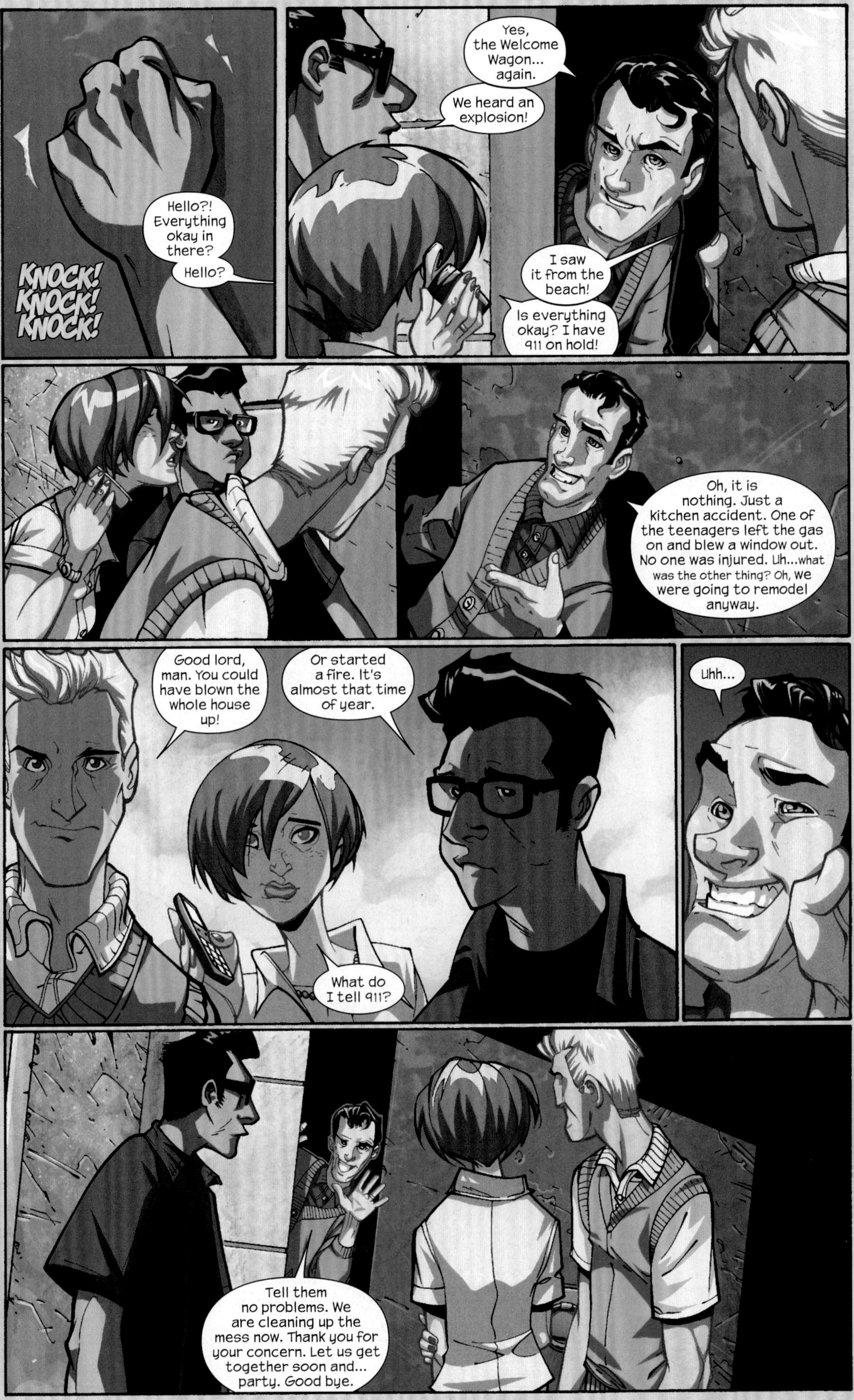
KNOCK! KNOCK! KNOCK!
Hello?! Everything okay in there?
Hello?
Yes, the Welcome Wagon... again.
We heard an explosion!
I saw it from the beach!
Is everything okay? I have 911 on hold!
Oh, it is nothing. Just a kitchen accident. One of the teenagers left the gas on and blew a window out. No one was injured. Uh...what was the other thing? Oh, we were going to remodel anyway.
Good lord, man. You could have blown the whole house up!
Or started a fire. It's almost that time of year.
What do I tell 911?
Uhh...
Tell them no problems. We are cleaning up the mess now. Thank you for your concern. Let us get together soon and... party. Good bye.

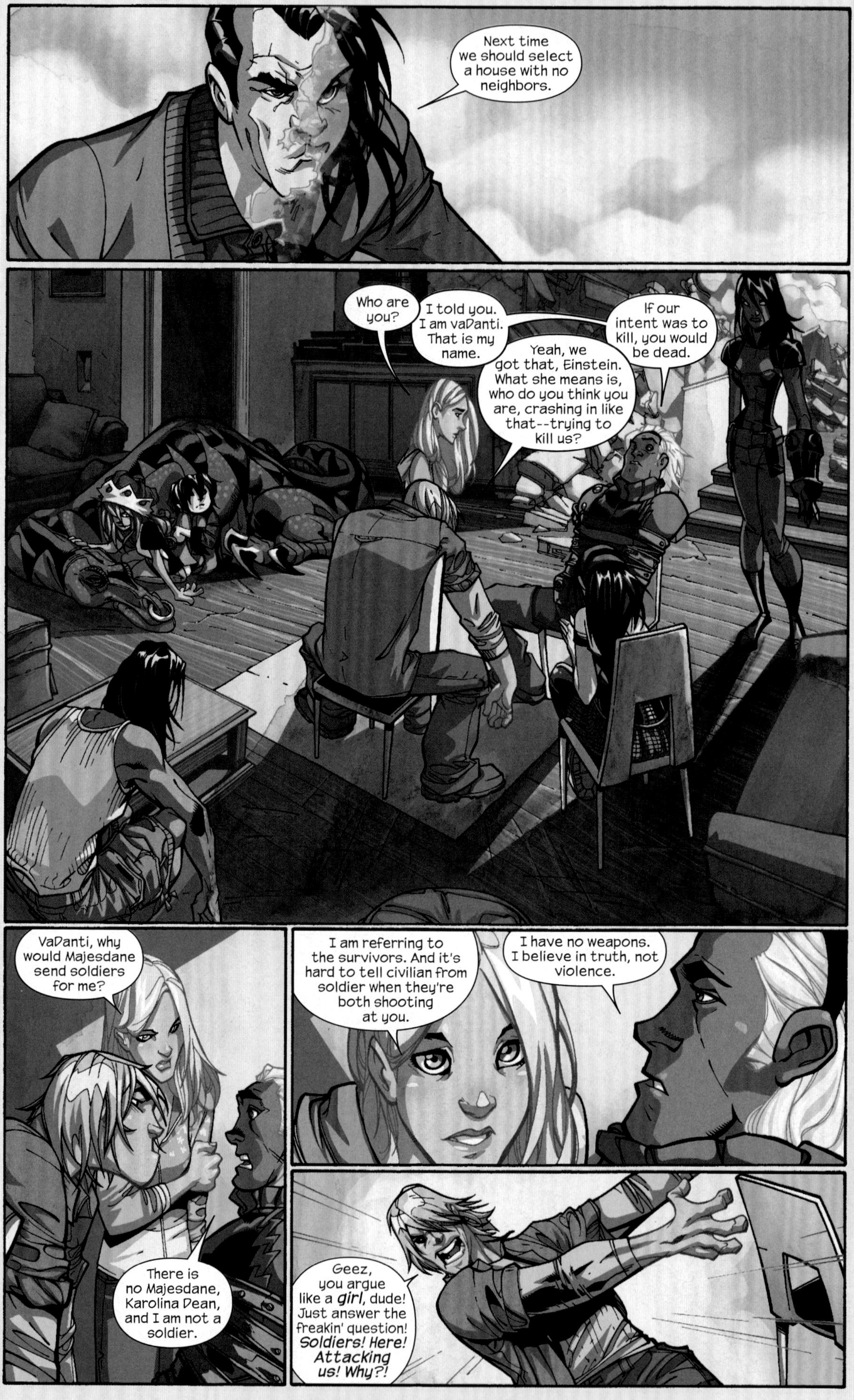
Next time we should select a house with no neighbors.
Who are you?
I told you. I am vaDanti. That is my name.
If our intent was to kill, you would be dead.
Yeah, we got that, Einstein. What she means is, who do you think you are, crashing in like that--trying to kill us?
VaDanti, why would Majesdane send soldiers for me?
There is no Majesdane, Karolina Dean, and I am not a soldier.
I am referring to the survivors. And it's hard to tell civilian from soldier when they're both shooting at you.
I have no weapons. I believe in truth, not violence.
Geez, you argue like a *girl*, dude! Just answer the freakin' question! *Soldiers! Here! Attacking us! Why?!*

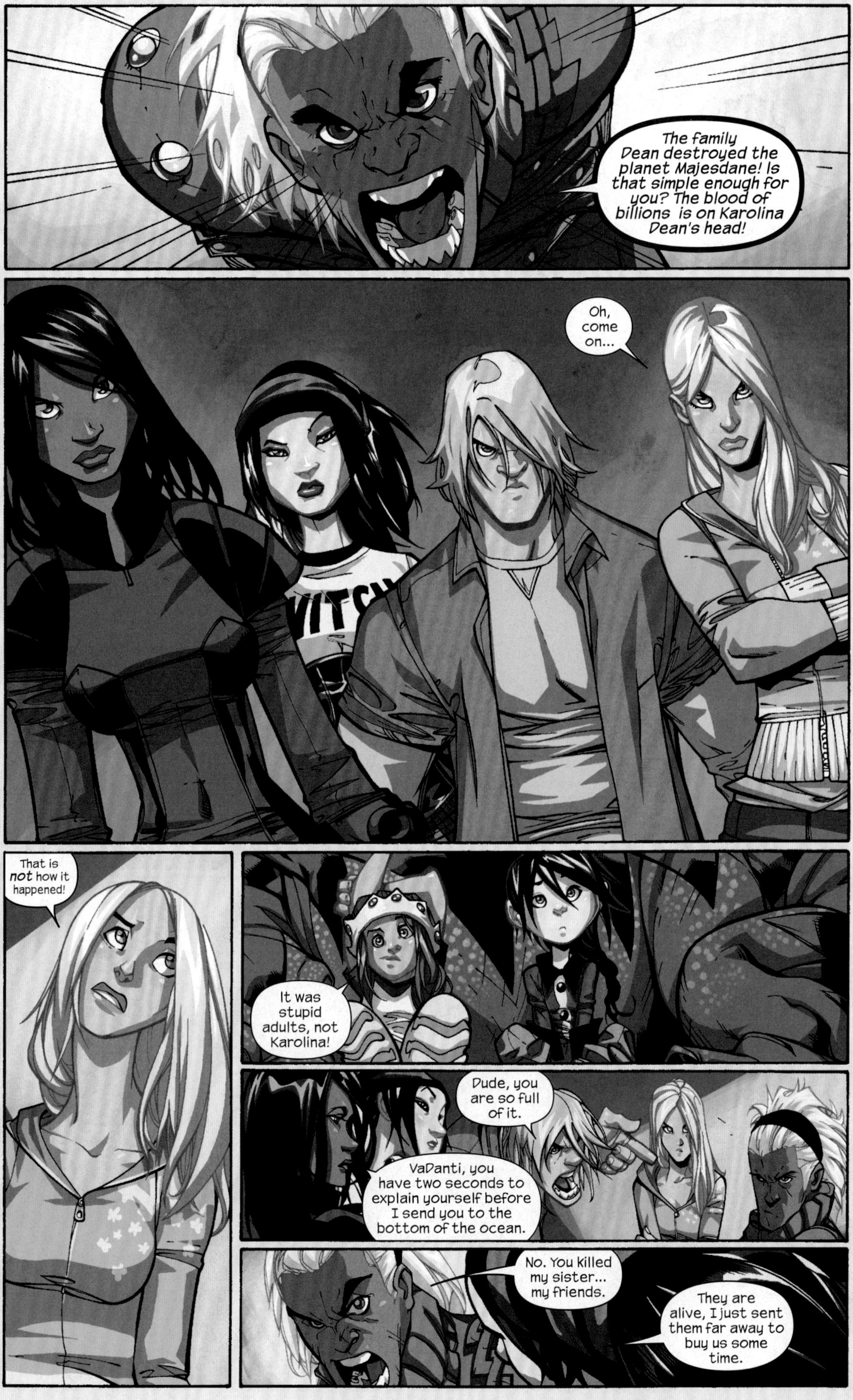
The family Dean destroyed the planet Majesdane! Is that simple enough for you? The blood of billions is on Karolina Dean's head!
Oh, come on...
WITC
That is **not** how it happened!
It was stupid adults, not Karolina!
Dude, you are so full of it.
VaDanti, you have two seconds to explain yourself before I send you to the bottom of the ocean.
No. You killed my sister... my friends.
They are alive, I just sent them far away to buy us some time.

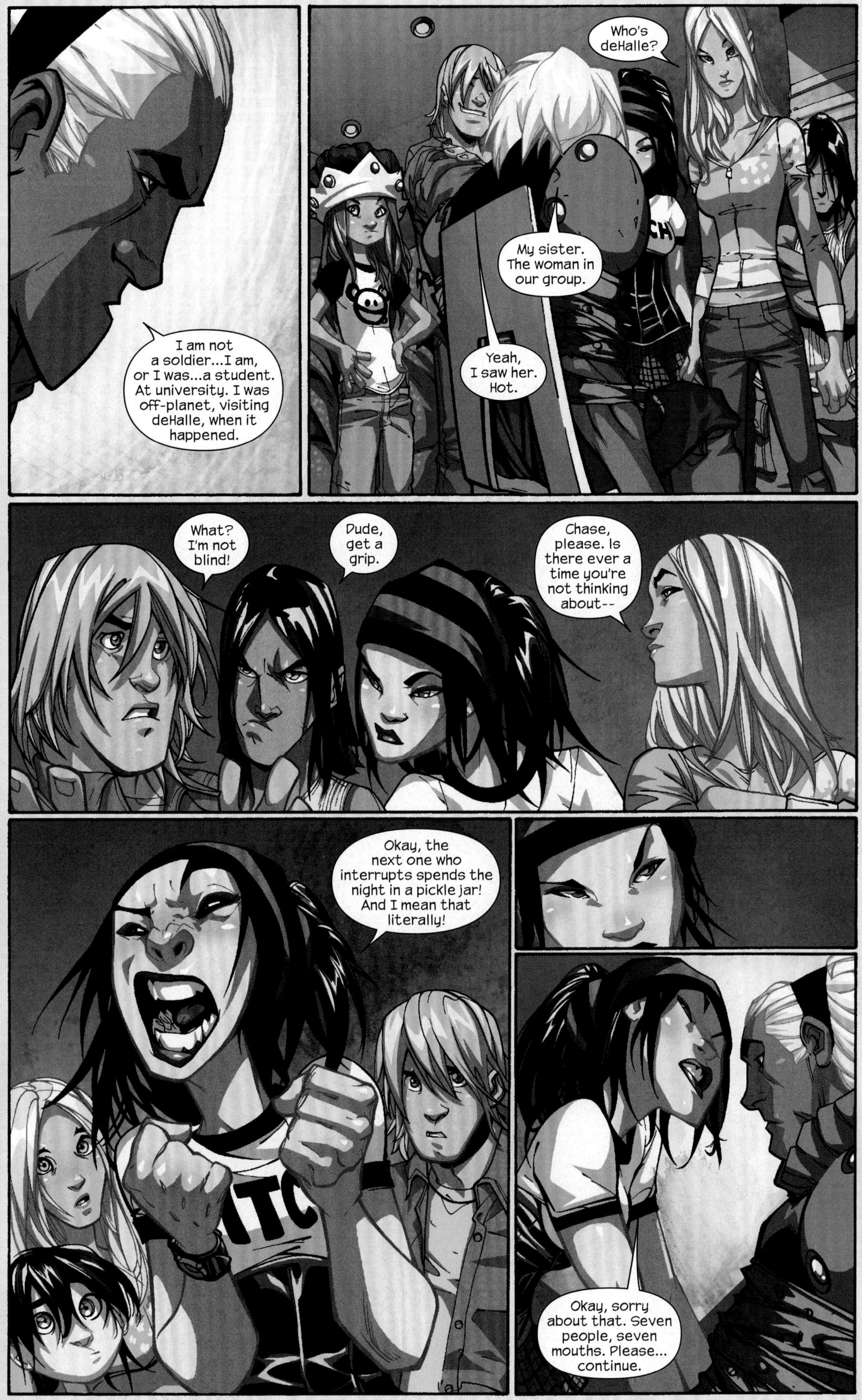
I am not a soldier...I am, or I was...a student. At university. I was off-planet, visiting deHalle, when it happened.
Who's deHalle?
My sister. The woman in our group.
Yeah, I saw her. Hot.
What? I'm not blind!
Dude, get a grip.
Chase, please. Is there ever a time you're not thinking about--
Okay, the next one who interrupts spends the night in a pickle jar! And I mean that literally!
Okay, sorry about that. Seven people, seven mouths. Please... continue.

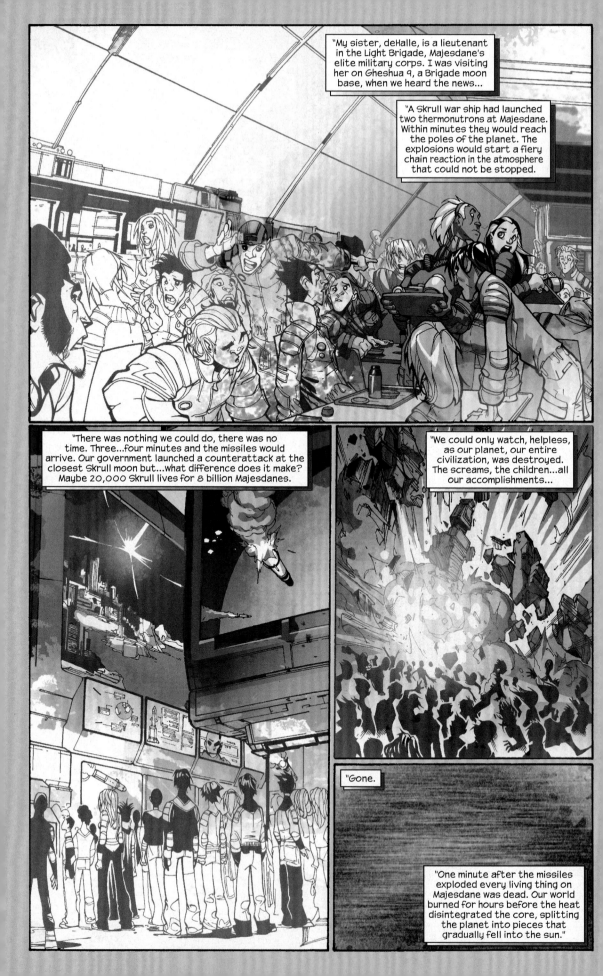

"My sister, deHalle, is a lieutenant in the Light Brigade, Majesdane's elite military corps. I was visiting her on Gheshua 9, a Brigade moon base, when we heard the news...

"A Skrull war ship had launched two thermonutrons at Majesdane. Within minutes they would reach the poles of the planet. The explosions would start a fiery chain reaction in the atmosphere that could not be stopped.

"There was nothing we could do, there was no time. Three...four minutes and the missiles would arrive. Our government launched a counterattack at the closest Skrull moon but...what difference does it make? Maybe 20,000 Skrull lives for 8 billion Majesdanes.

"We could only watch, helpless, as our planet, our entire civilization, was destroyed. The screams, the children...all our accomplishments...

"Gone.

"One minute after the missiles exploded every living thing on Majesdane was dead. Our world burned for hours before the heat disintegrated the core, splitting the planet into pieces that gradually fell into the sun."

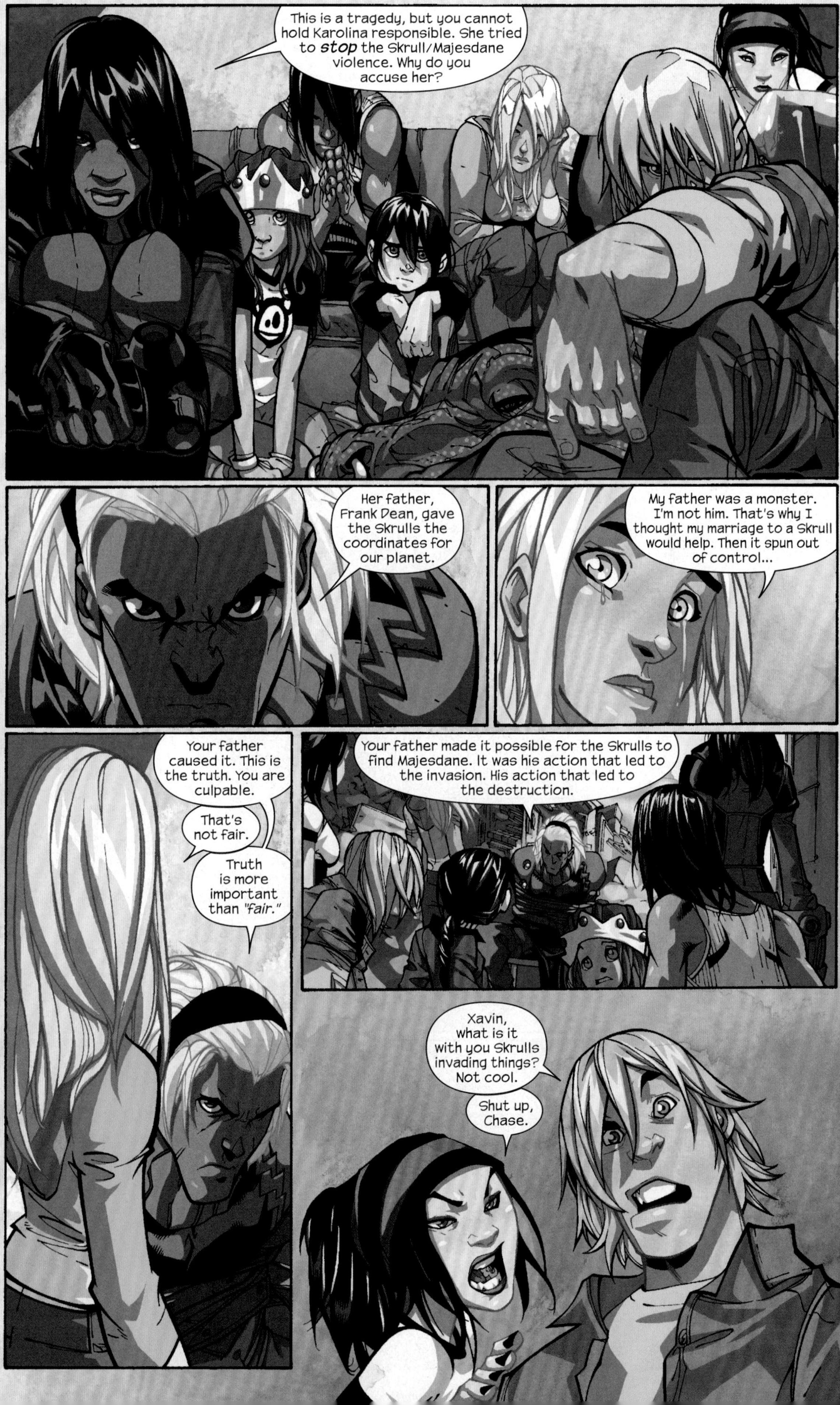
This is a tragedy, but you cannot hold Karolina responsible. She tried to *stop* the Skrull/Majesdane violence. Why do you accuse her?
Her father, Frank Dean, gave the Skrulls the coordinates for our planet.
My father was a monster. I'm not him. That's why I thought my marriage to a Skrull would help. Then it spun out of control...
Your father caused it. This is the truth. You are culpable.
That's not fair.
Truth is more important than "fair."
Your father made it possible for the Skrulls to find Majesdane. It was his action that led to the invasion. His action that led to the destruction.
Xavin, what is it with you Skrulls invading things? Not cool.
Shut up, Chase.

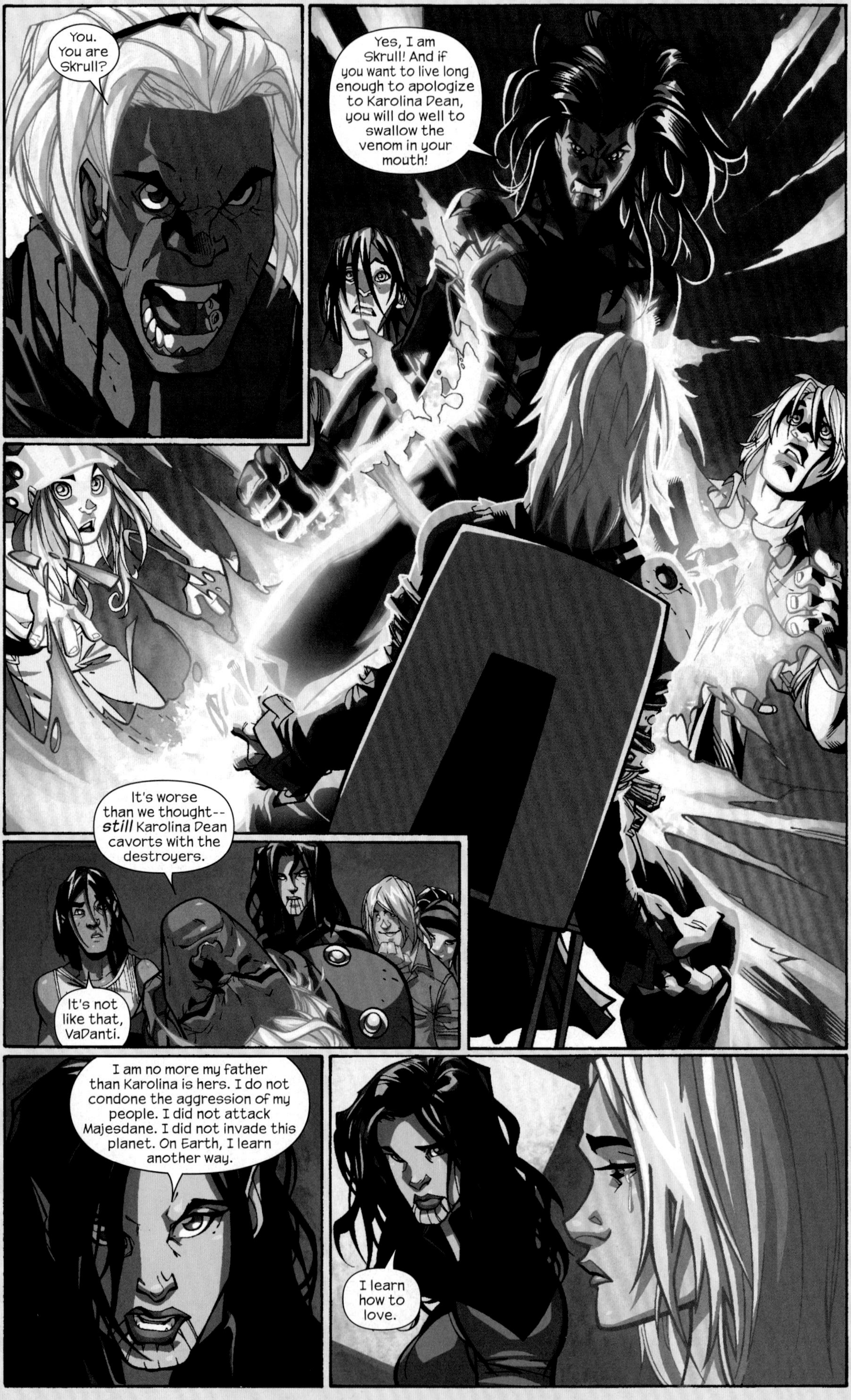
You. You are Skrull?
Yes, I am Skrull! And if you want to live long enough to apologize to Karolina Dean, you will do well to swallow the venom in your mouth!
It's worse than we thought-- ***still*** Karolina Dean cavorts with the destroyers.
It's not like that, VaDanti.
I am no more my father than Karolina is hers. I do not condone the aggression of my people. I did not attack Majesdane. I did not invade this planet. On Earth, I learn another way.
I learn how to love.

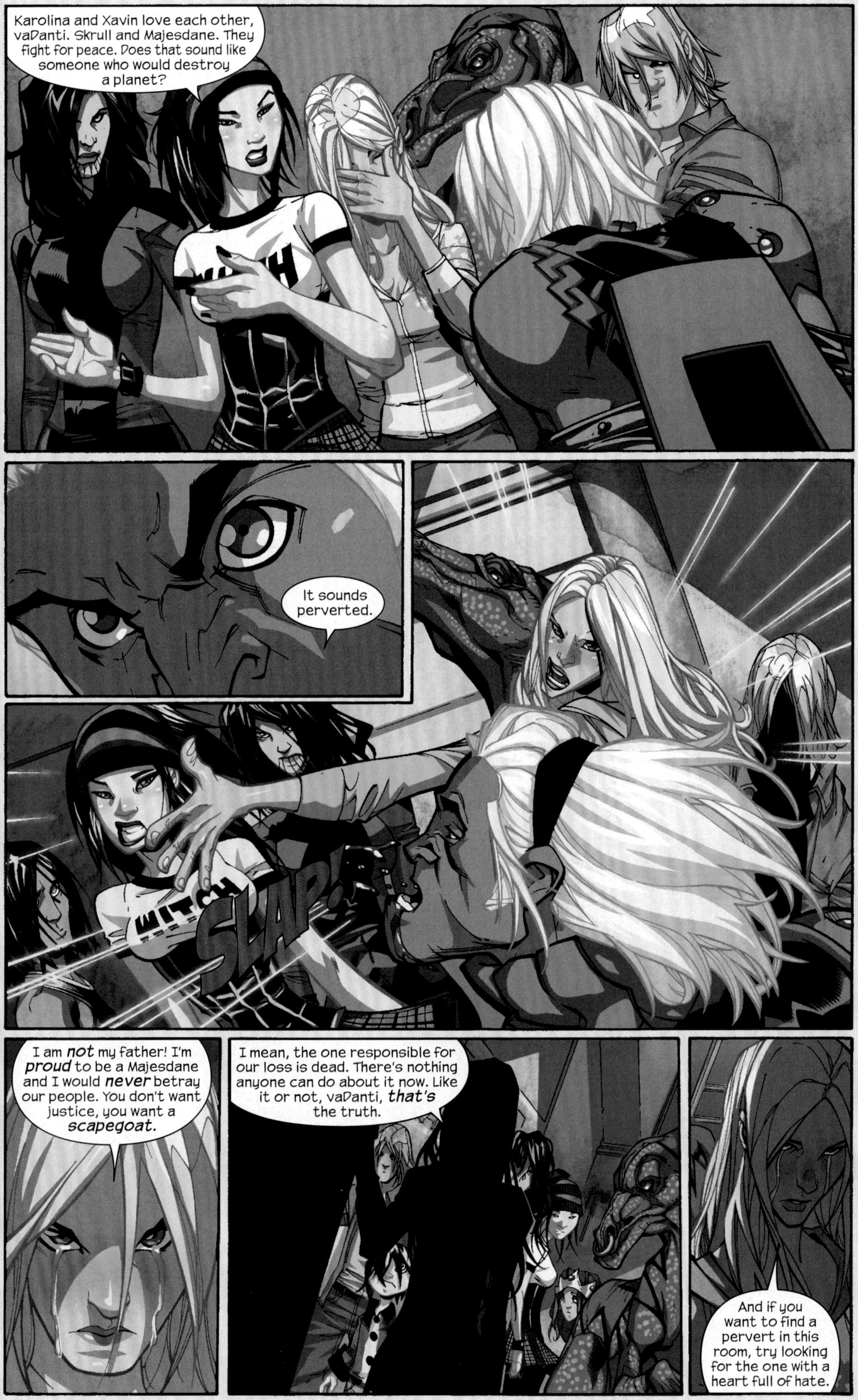
Karolina and Xavin love each other, vaDanti. Skrull and Majesdane. They fight for peace. Does that sound like someone who would destroy a planet?
WITCH
It sounds perverted.
WITCH
SLAP!
I am *not* my father! I'm *proud* to be a Majesdane and I would *never* betray our people. You don't want justice, you want a *scapegoat.*
I mean, the one responsible for our loss is dead. There's nothing anyone can do about it now. Like it or not, vaDanti, *that's* the truth.
And if you want to find a pervert in this room, try looking for the one with a heart full of hate.

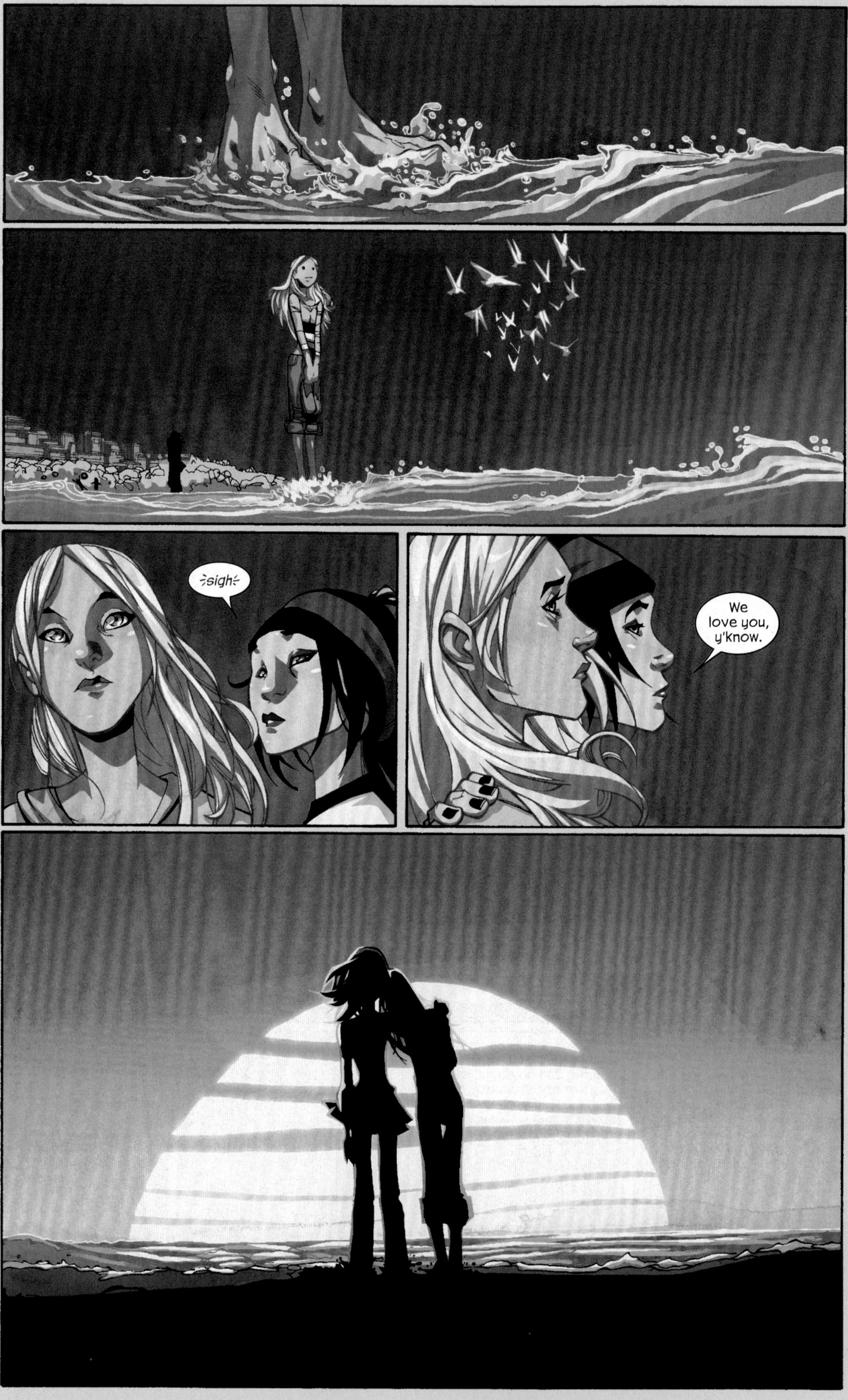
sigh
We love you, y'know.

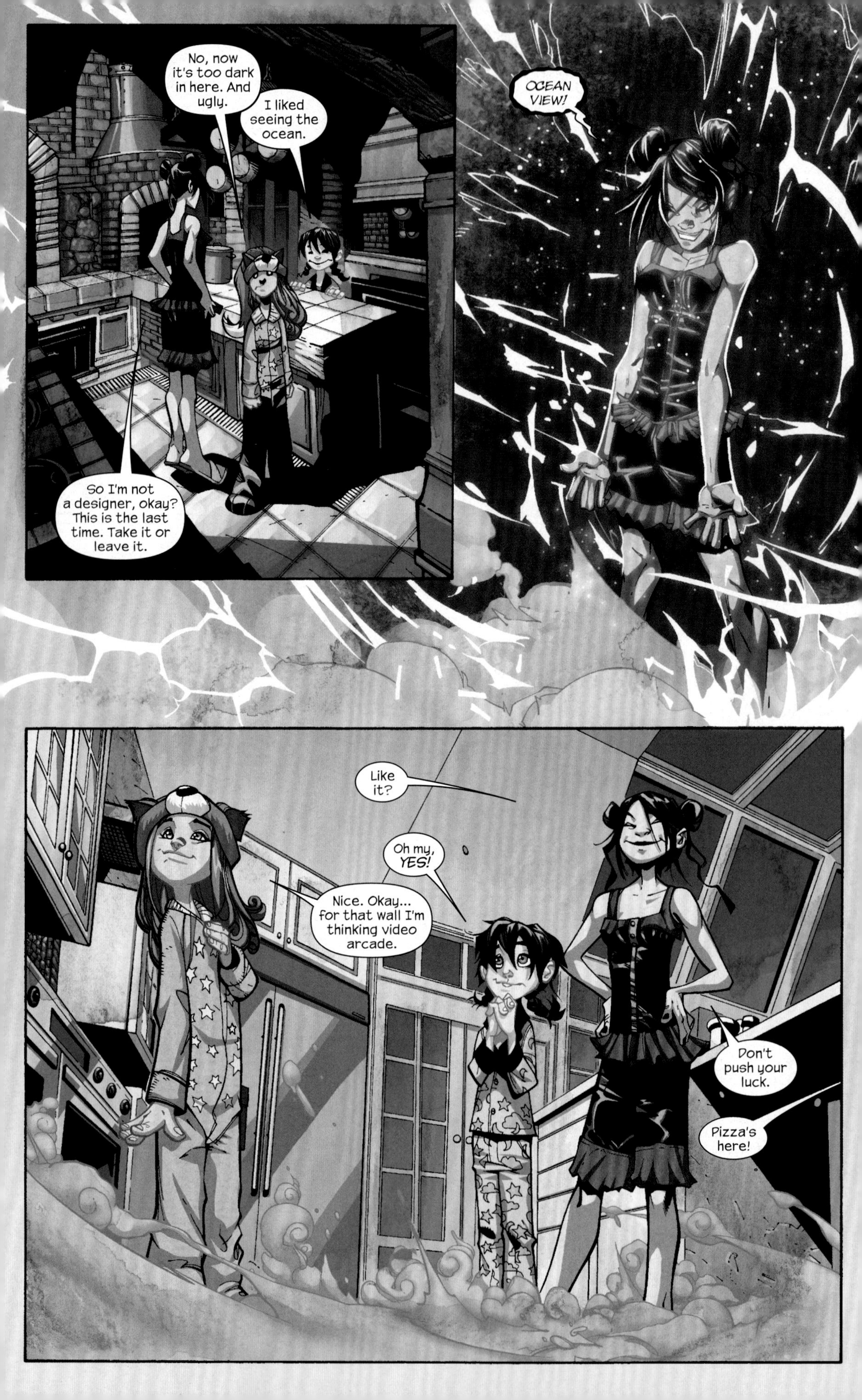
No, now it's too dark in here. And ugly.
I liked seeing the ocean.
So I'm not a designer, okay? This is the last time. Take it or leave it.
OCEAN VIEW!
Like it?
Oh my, YES!
Nice. Okay... for that wall I'm thinking video arcade.
Don't push your luck.
Pizza's here!

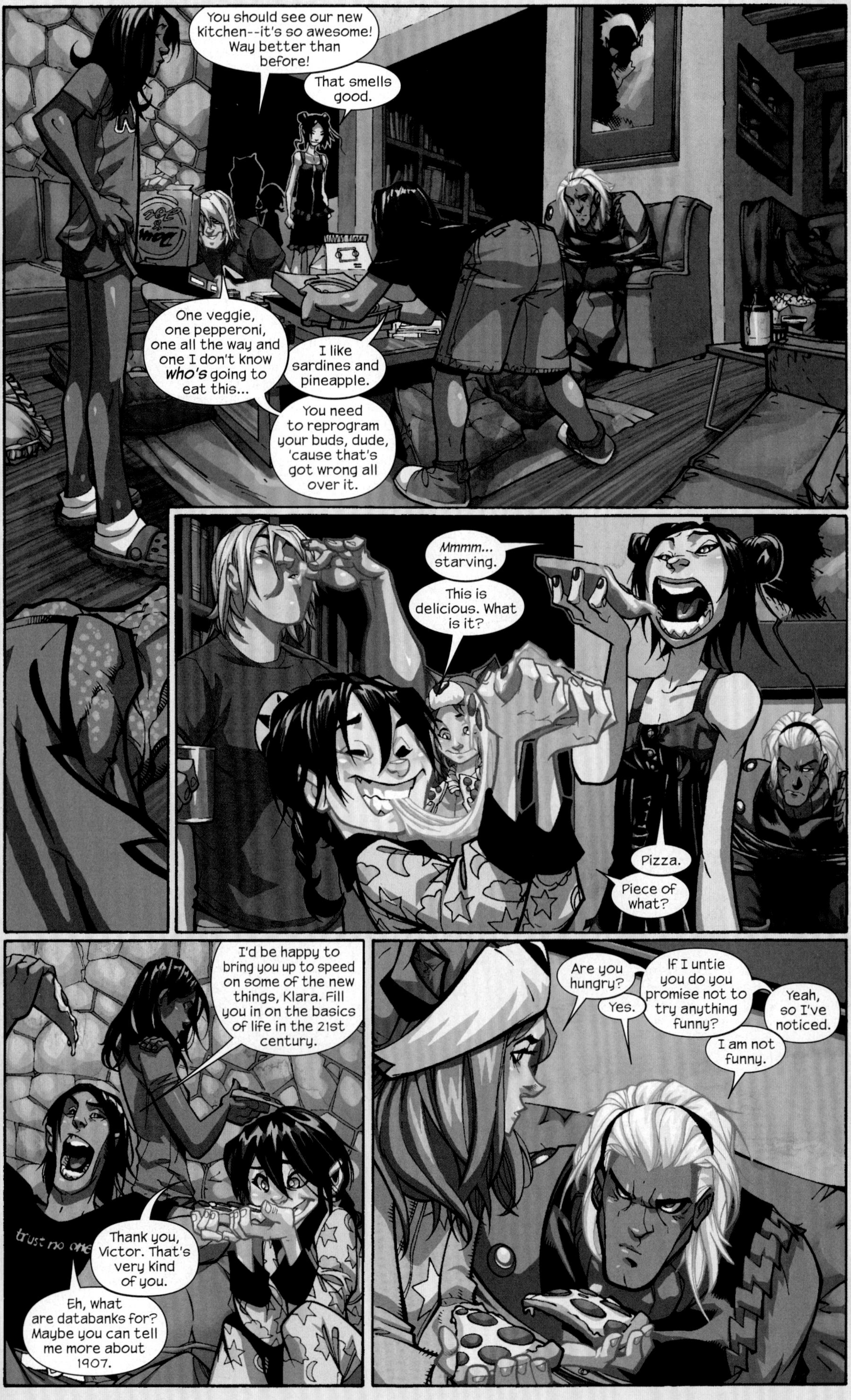
You should see our new kitchen--it's so awesome! Way better than before!
That smells good.
One veggie, one pepperoni, one all the way and one I don't know *who's* going to eat this...
I like sardines and pineapple.
You need to reprogram your buds, dude, 'cause that's got wrong all over it.
*Mmmm...* starving.
This is delicious. What is it?
Pizza.
Piece of what?
I'd be happy to bring you up to speed on some of the new things, Klara. Fill you in on the basics of life in the 21st century.
trust no one
Thank you, Victor. That's very kind of you.
Eh, what are databanks for? Maybe you can tell me more about 1907.
Are you hungry?
Yes.
If I untie you do you promise not to try anything funny?
I am not funny.
Yeah, so I've noticed.

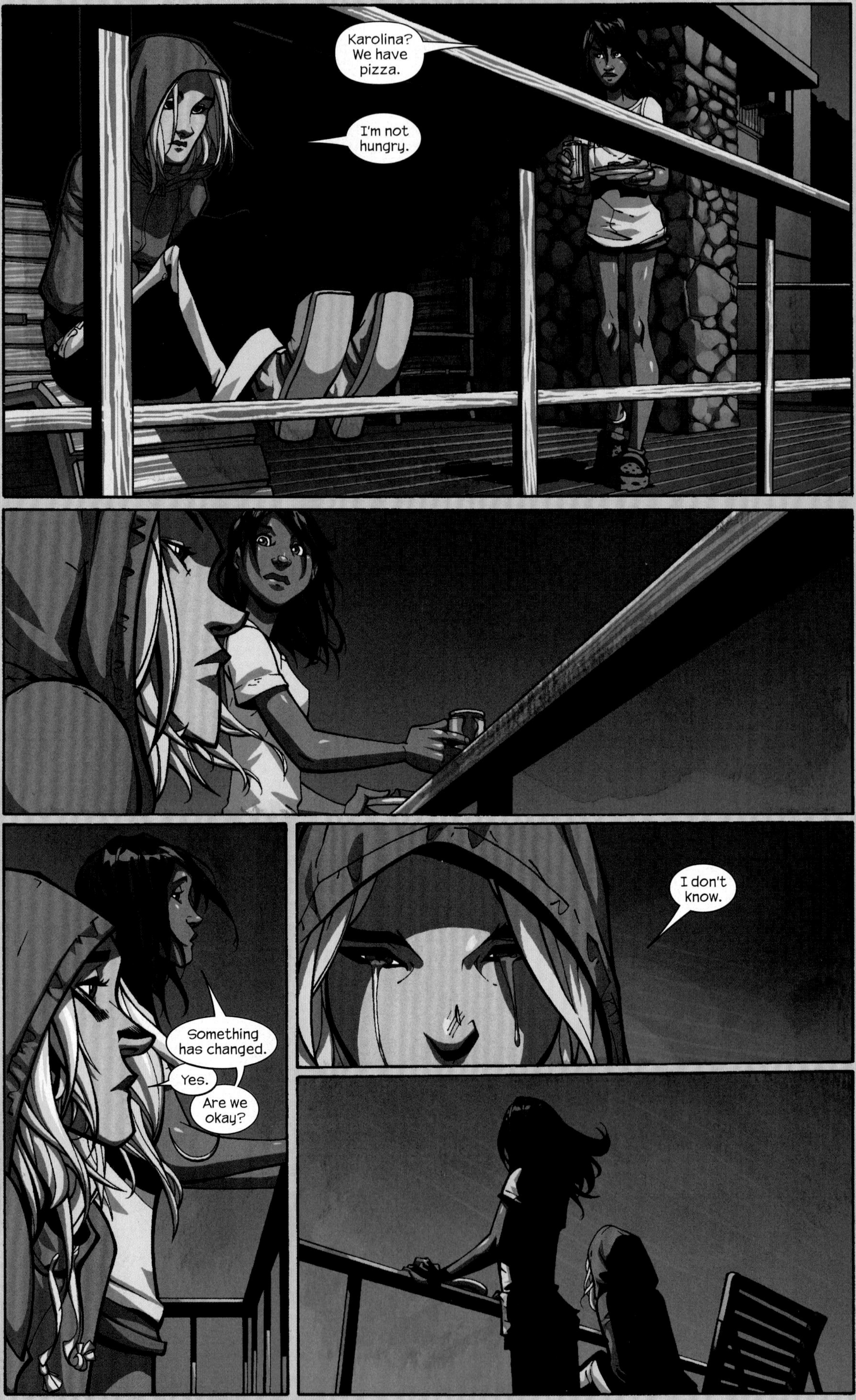
Karolina? We have pizza.
I'm not hungry.
Something has changed.
Yes.
Are we okay?
I don't know.

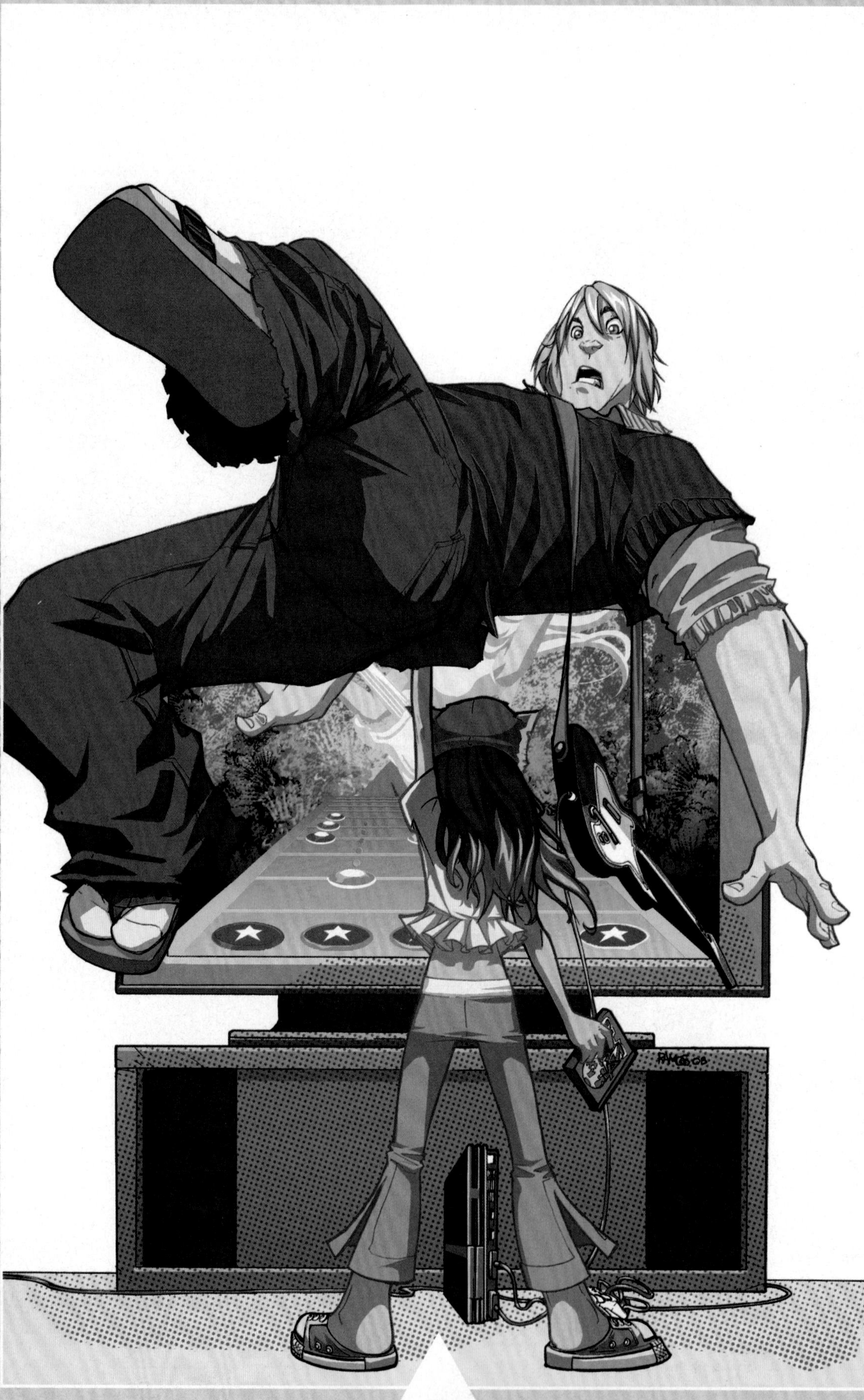

3

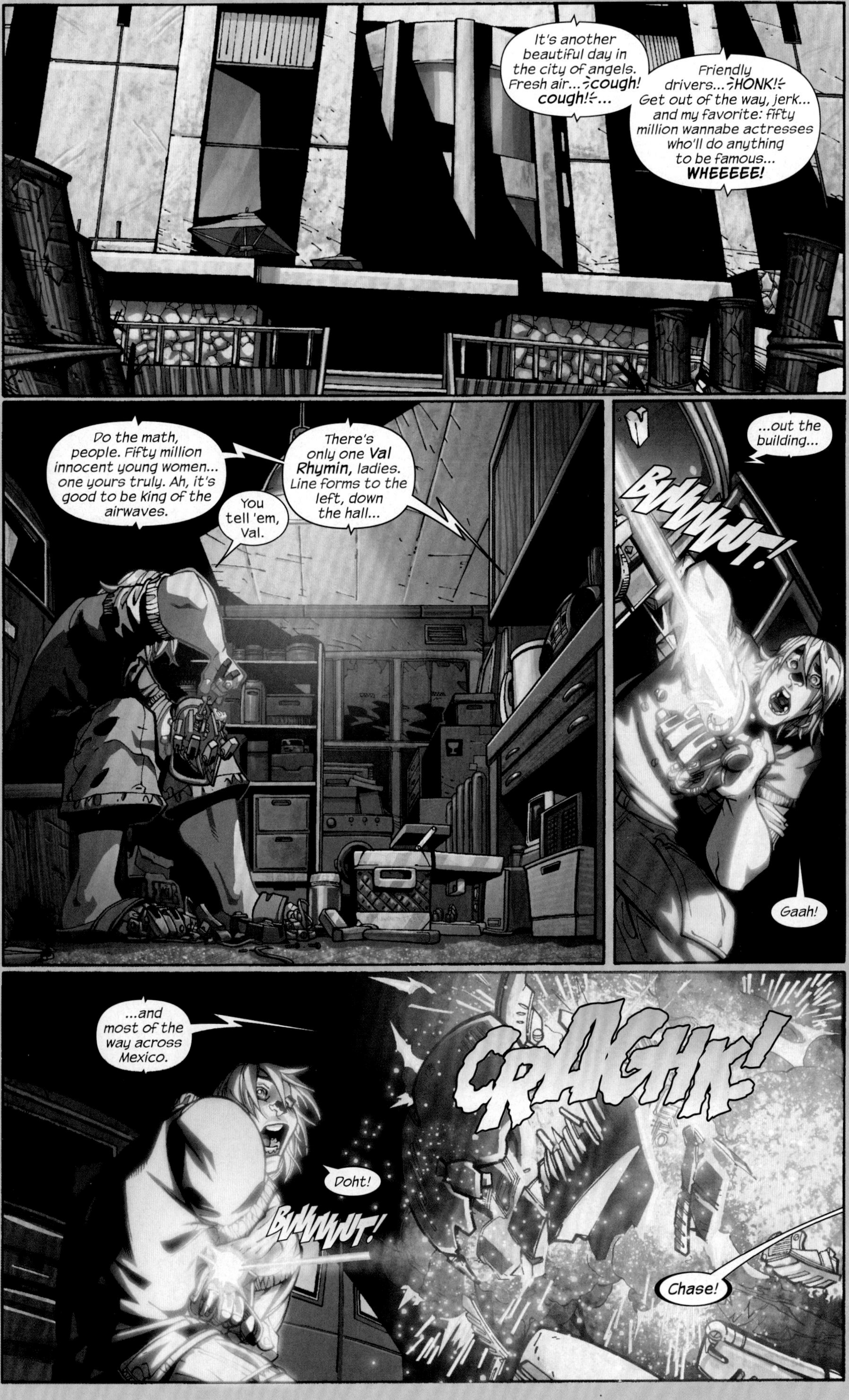

It's another beautiful day in the city of angels. Fresh air... cough! cough!...
Friendly drivers... HONK! Get out of the way, jerk... and my favorite: fifty million wannabe actresses who'll do anything to be famous... WHEEEEE!
Do the math, people. Fifty million innocent young women... one yours truly. Ah, it's good to be king of the airwaves.
You tell 'em, Val.
There's only one Val Rhymin, ladies. Line forms to the left, down the hall...
...out the building...
BWWWJUT!
Gaah!
...and most of the way across Mexico.
CRAGHK!
Doht!
BWWWJUT!
Chase!

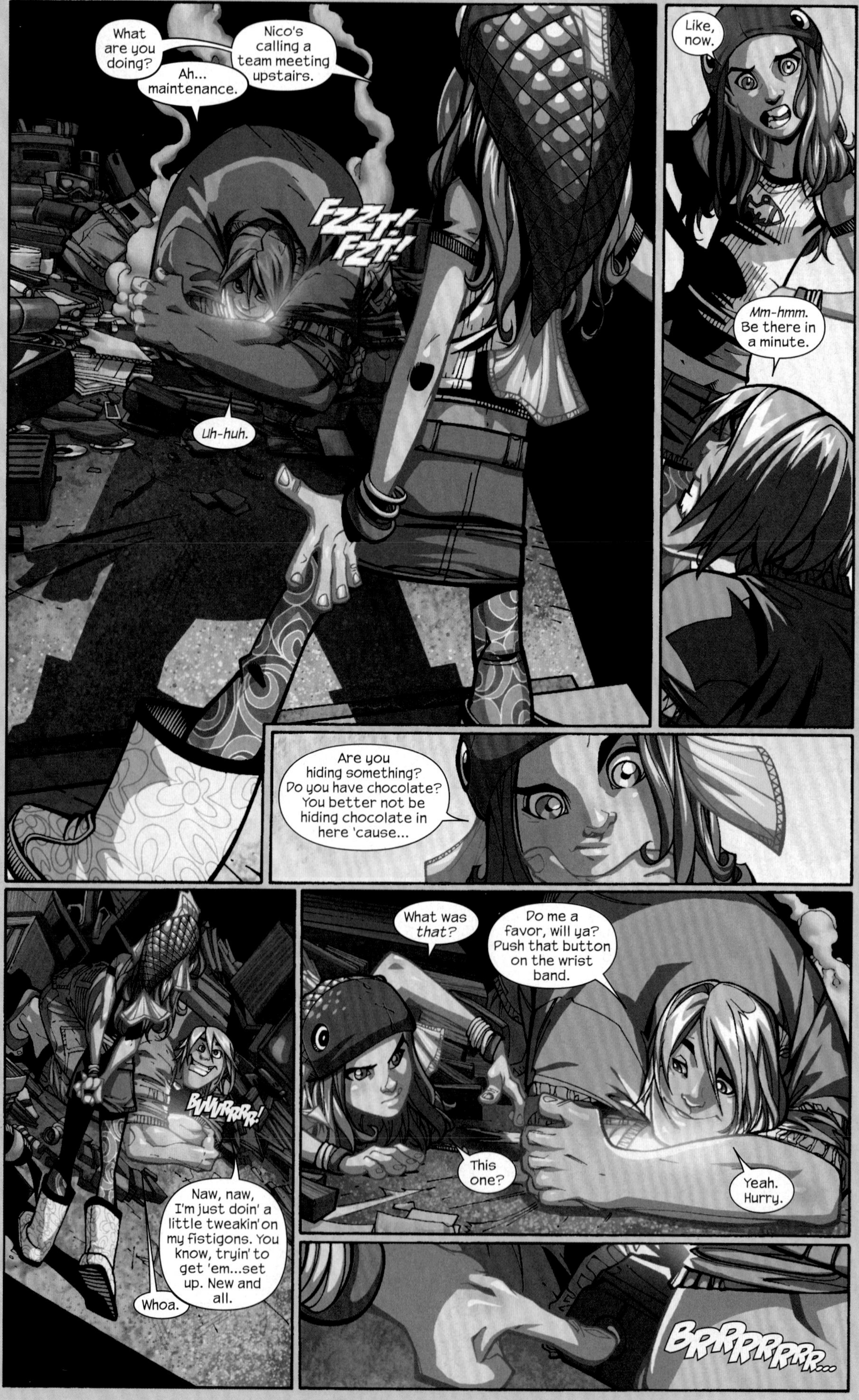
What are you doing?
Nico's calling a team meeting upstairs.
Ah... maintenance.
FZZT! FZT!
Uh-huh.
Like, now.
Mm-hmm. Be there in a minute.
Are you hiding something? Do you have chocolate? You better not be hiding chocolate in here 'cause...
BUWRRRR!
Whoa.
Naw, naw, I'm just doin' a little tweakin' on my fistigons. You know, tryin' to get 'em...set up. New and all.
What was that?
Do me a favor, will ya? Push that button on the wrist band.
This one?
Yeah. Hurry.
BRRRRRRRR...

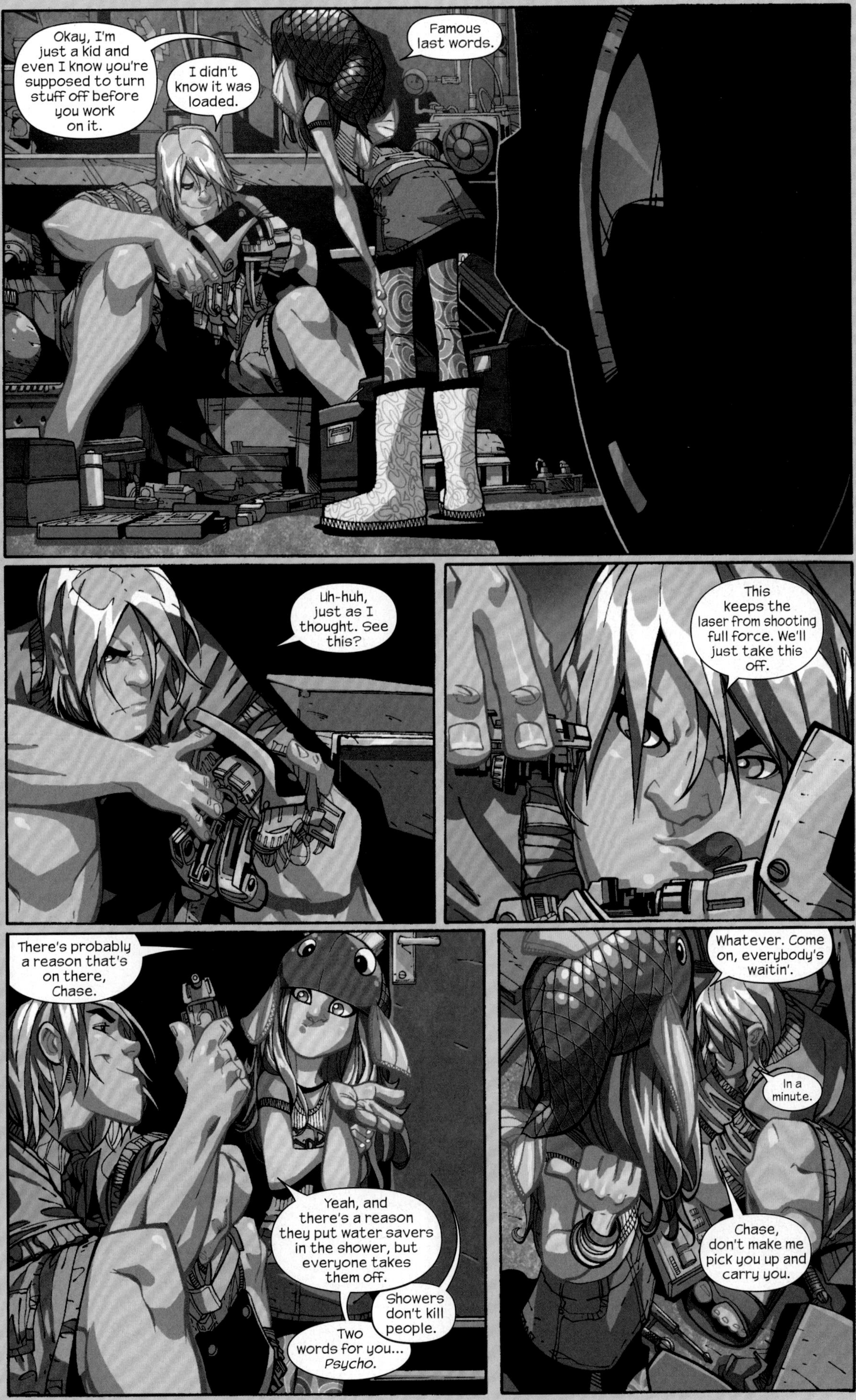
Okay, I'm just a kid and even I know you're supposed to turn stuff off before you work on it.
I didn't know it was loaded.
Famous last words.
Uh-huh, just as I thought. See this?
This keeps the laser from shooting full force. We'll just take this off.
There's probably a reason that's on there, Chase.
Yeah, and there's a reason they put water savers in the shower, but everyone takes them off.
Showers don't kill people.
Two words for you... *Psycho*.
Whatever. Come on, everybody's waitin'.
In a minute.
Chase, don't make me pick you up and carry you.

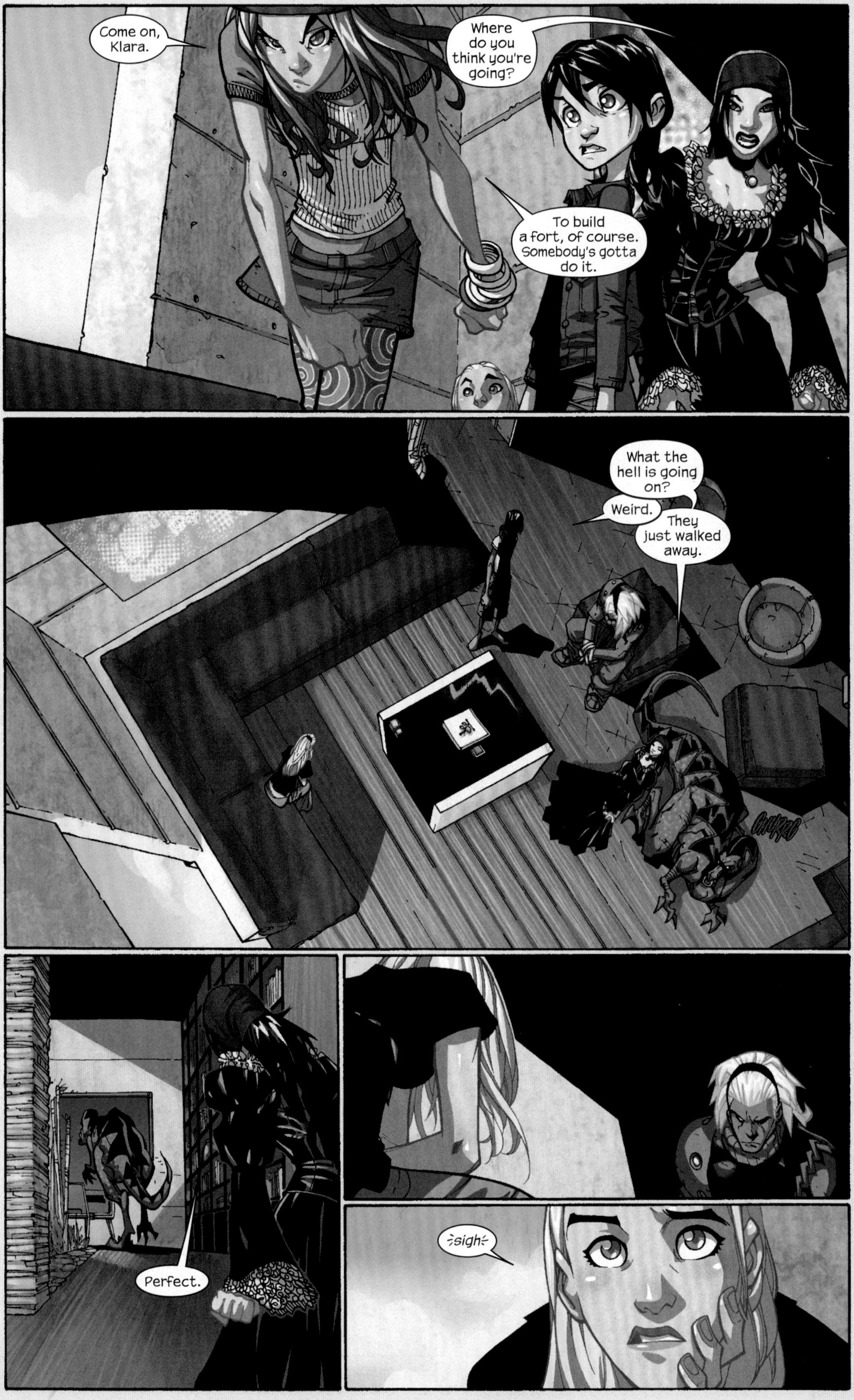
Come on, Klara.
Where do you think you're going?
To build a fort, of course. Somebody's gotta do it.
What the hell is going on?
Weird.
They just walked away.
Perfect.
~sigh~

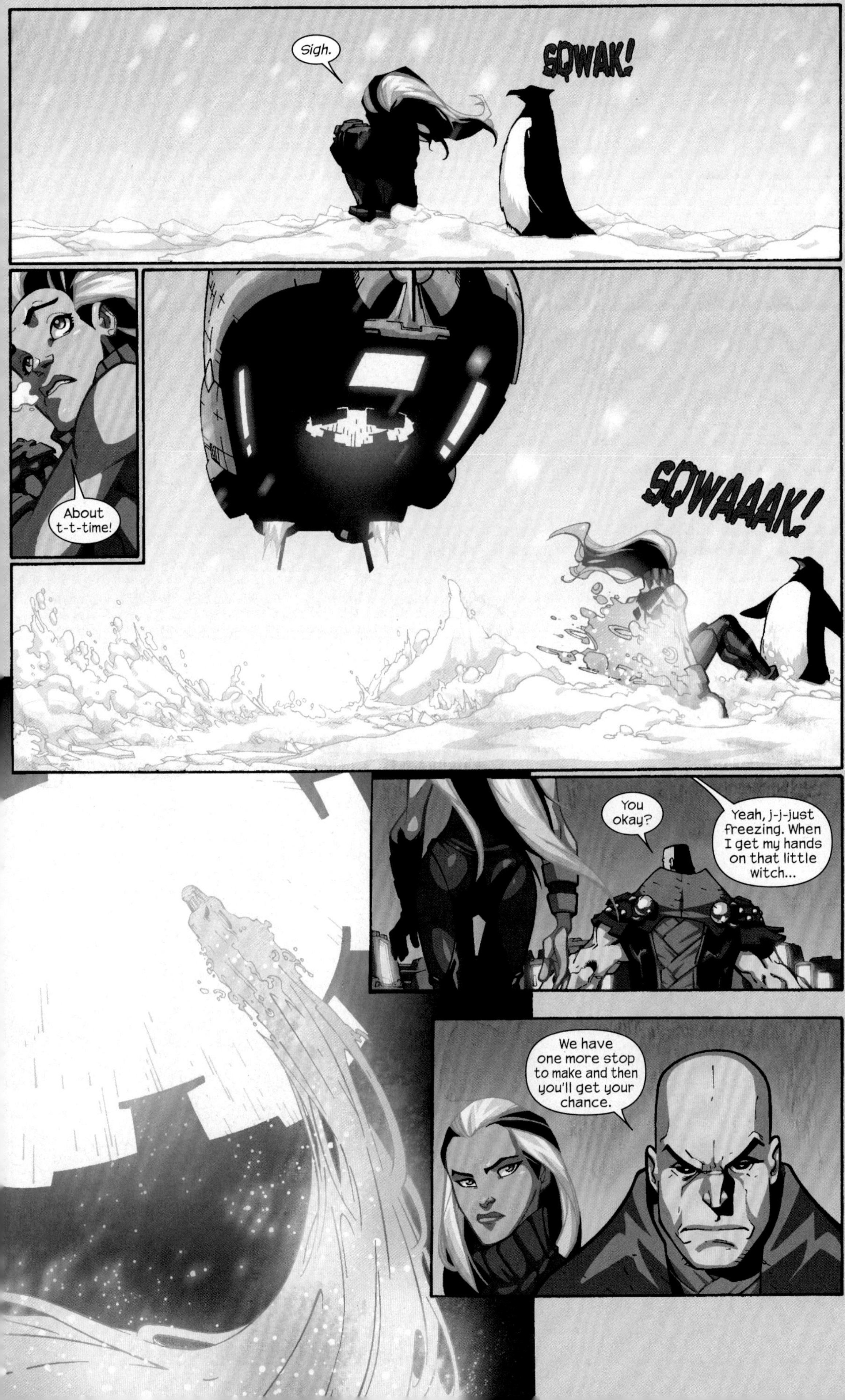

Sigh.
SQWAK!
About t-t-time!
SQWAAAK!
You okay?
Yeah, j-j-just freezing. When I get my hands on that little witch...
We have one more stop to make and then you'll get your chance.

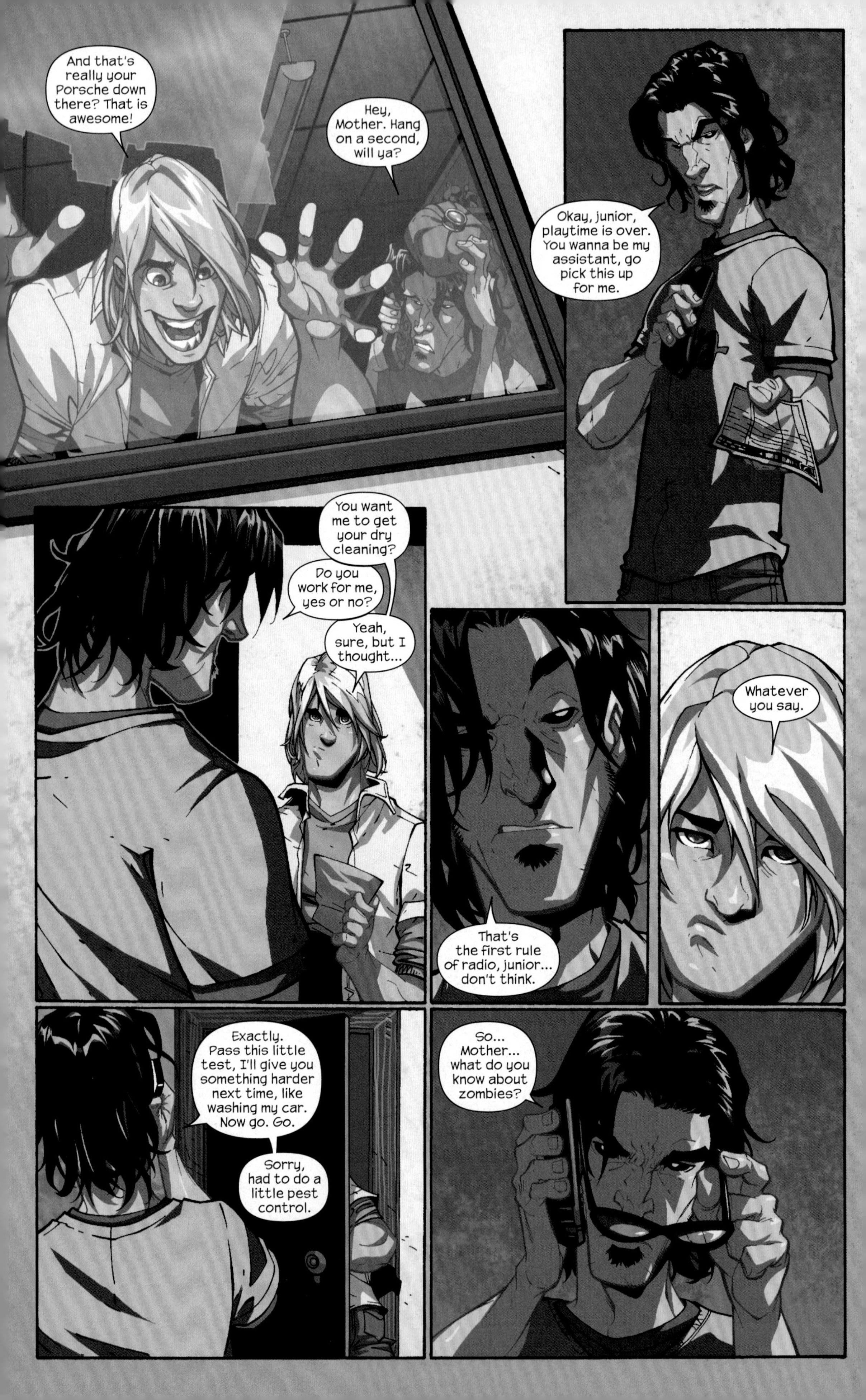

And that's really your Porsche down there? That is awesome!
Hey, Mother. Hang on a second, will ya?
Okay, junior, playtime is over. You wanna be my assistant, go pick this up for me.
You want me to get your dry cleaning?
Do you work for me, yes or no?
Yeah, sure, but I thought...
That's the first rule of radio, junior... don't think.
Whatever you say.
Exactly. Pass this little test, I'll give you something harder next time, like washing my car. Now go. Go.
Sorry, had to do a little pest control.
So... Mother... what do you know about zombies?

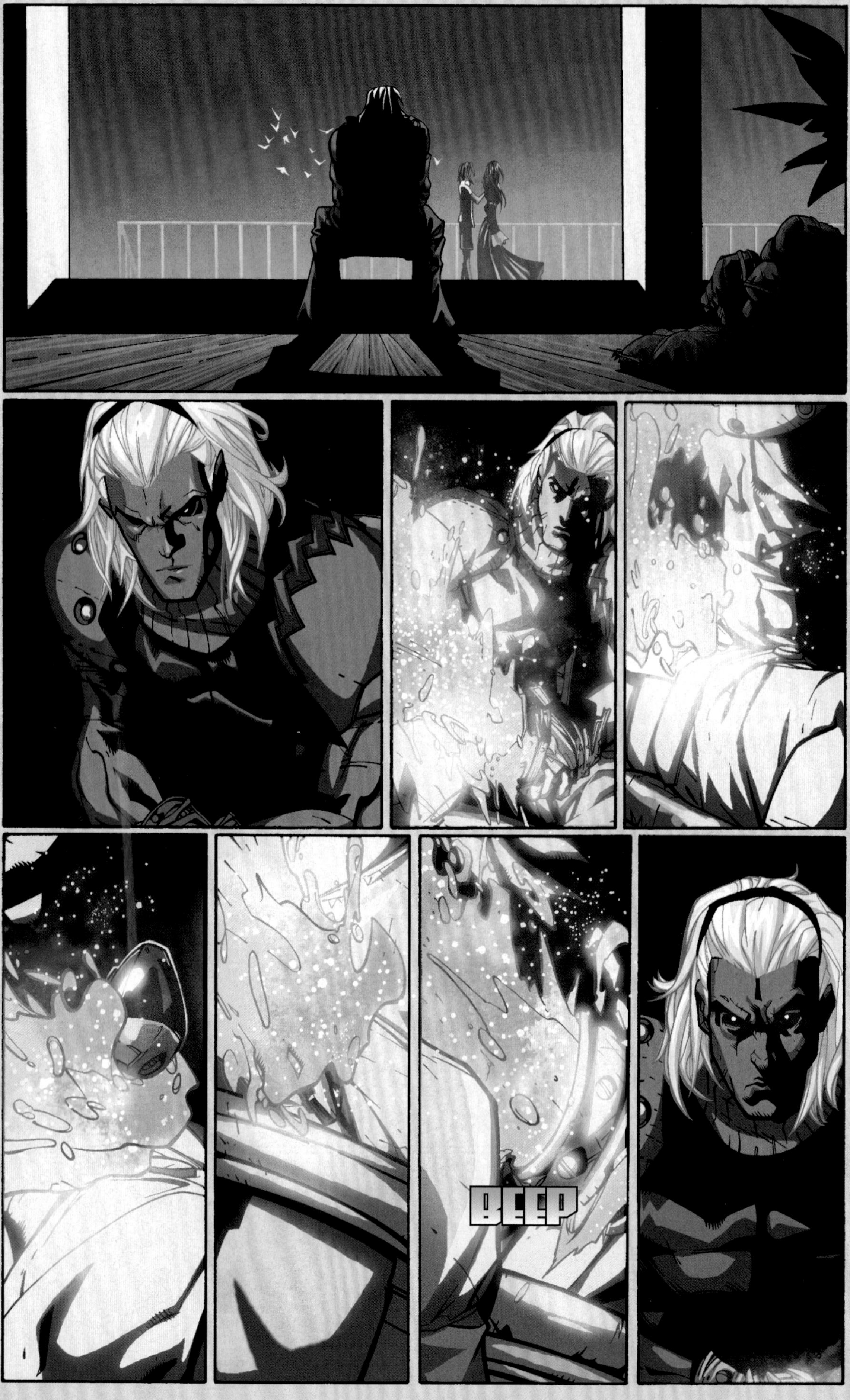
BEEP

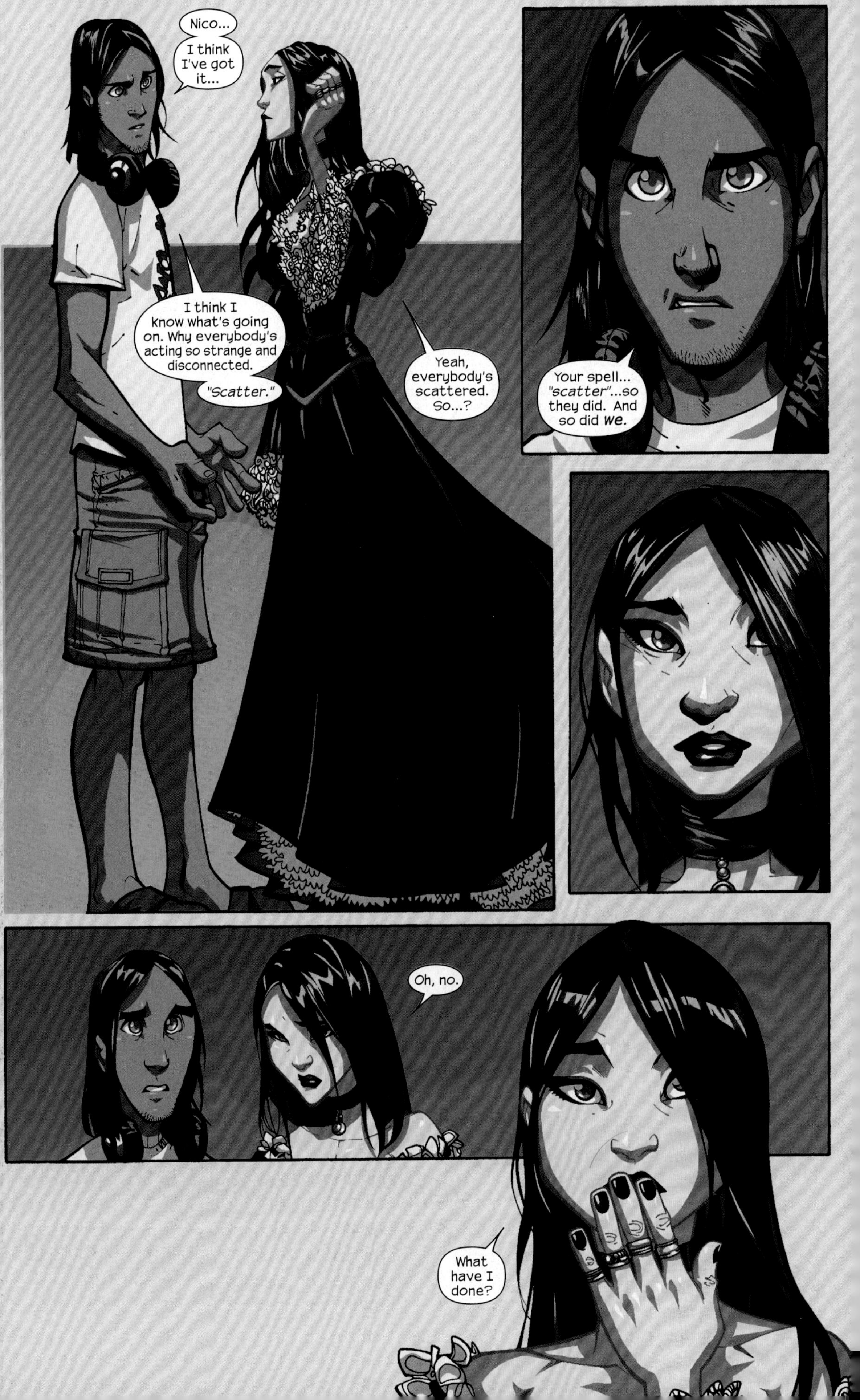
Nico... I think I've got it...
I think I know what's going on. Why everybody's acting so strange and disconnected.
"Scatter."
Yeah, everybody's scattered. So...?
Your spell... "scatter"...so they did. And so did we.
Oh, no.
What have I done?

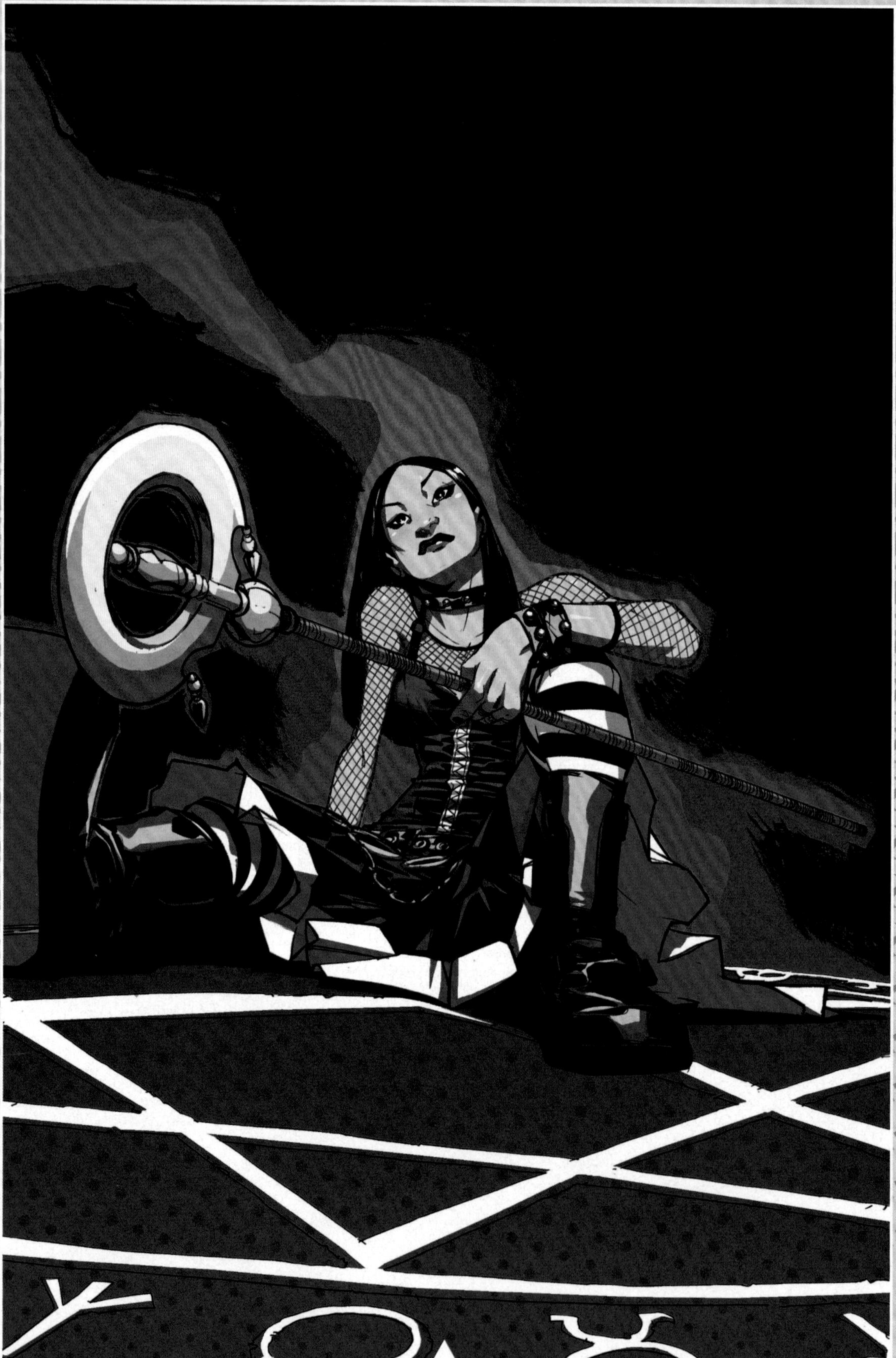

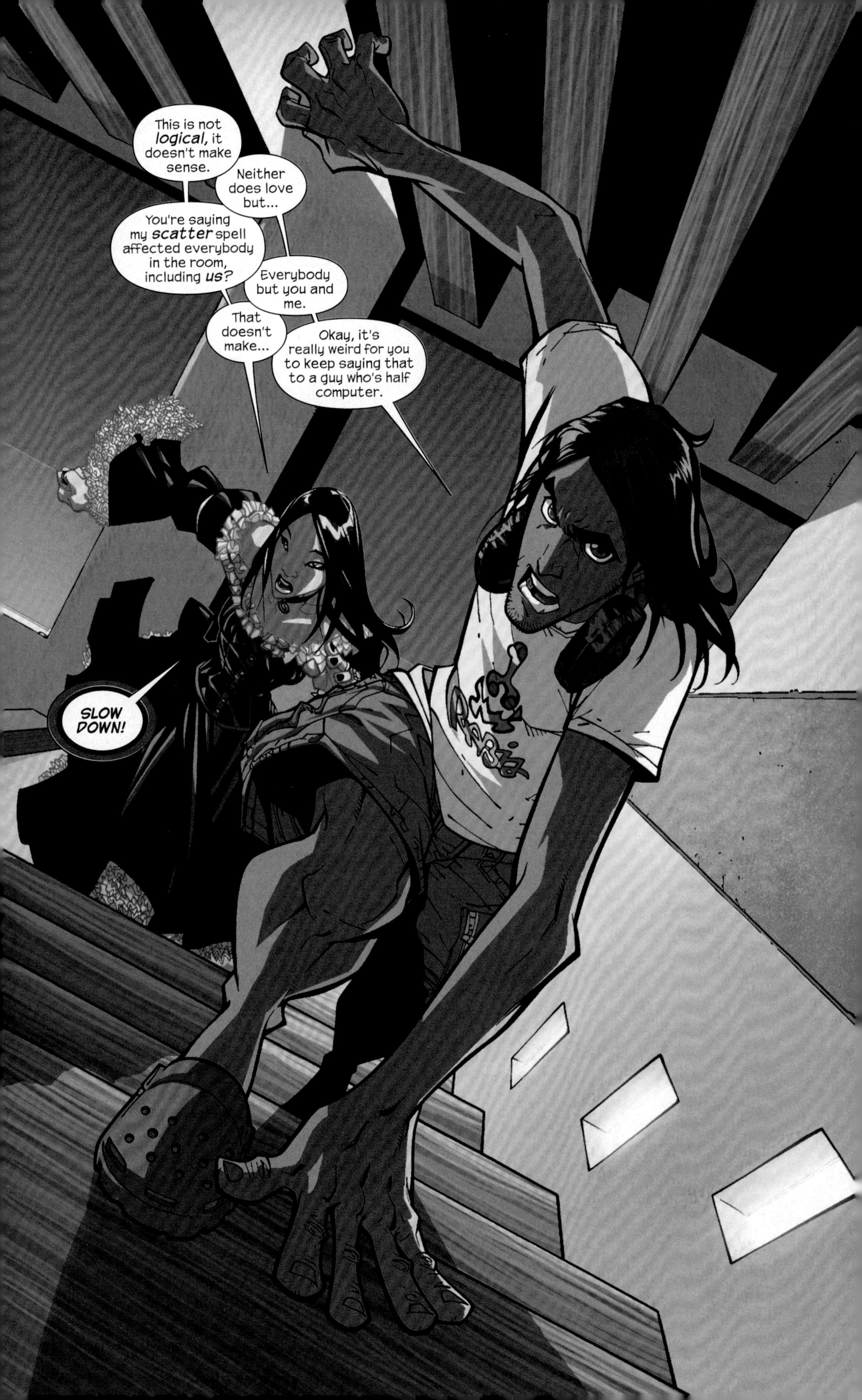
This is not *logical,* it doesn't make sense.
Neither does love but...
You're saying my **scatter** spell affected everybody in the room, including *us?*
Everybody but you and me.
That doesn't make...
Okay, it's really weird for you to keep saying that to a guy who's half computer.
SLOW DOWN!

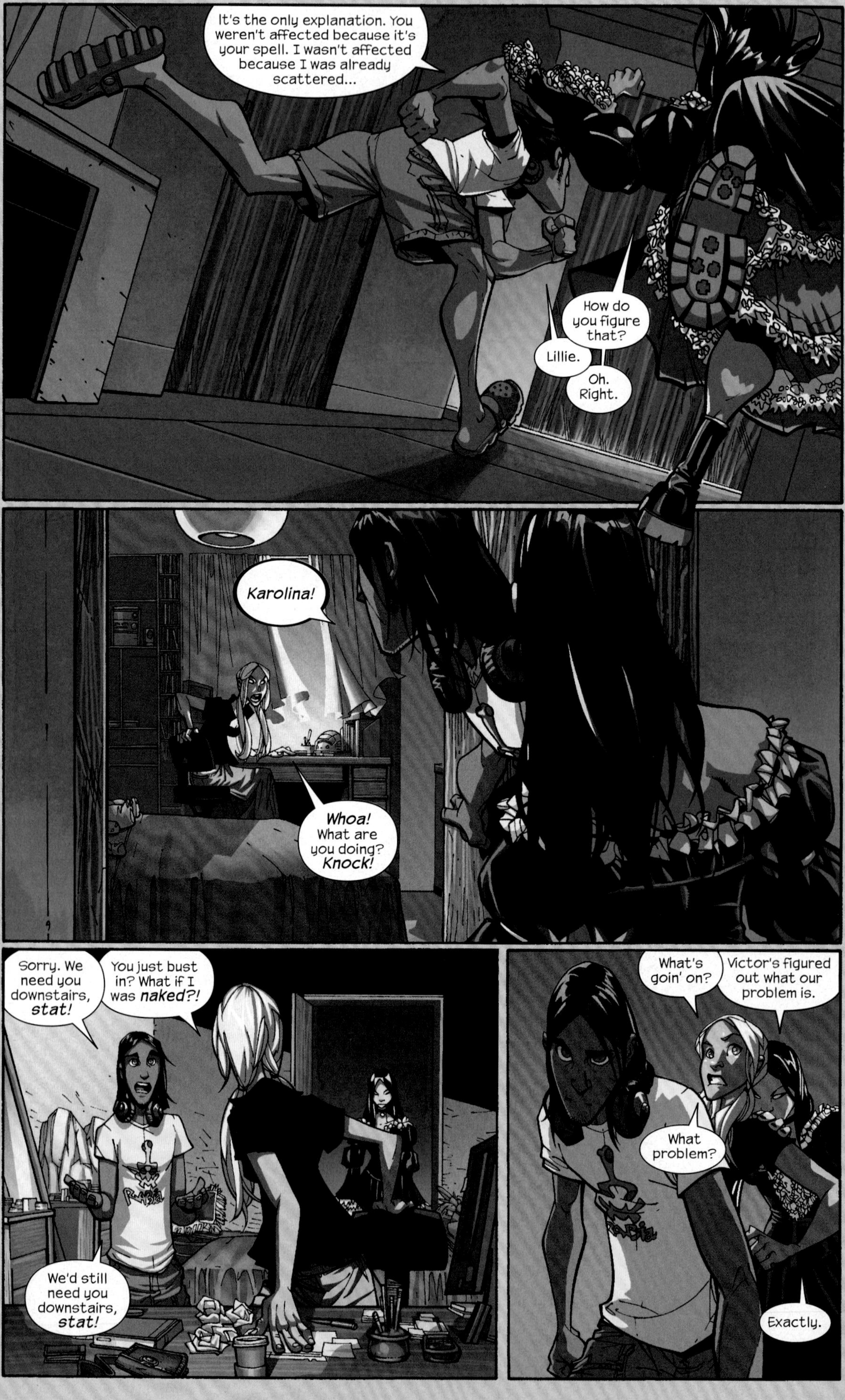
It's the only explanation. You weren't affected because it's your spell. I wasn't affected because I was already scattered...
How do you figure that?
Lillie.
Oh. Right.
Karolina!
Whoa! What are you doing? Knock!
Sorry. We need you downstairs, stat!
You just bust in? What if I was naked?!
We'd still need you downstairs, stat!
What's goin' on?
Victor's figured out what our problem is.
What problem?
Exactly.

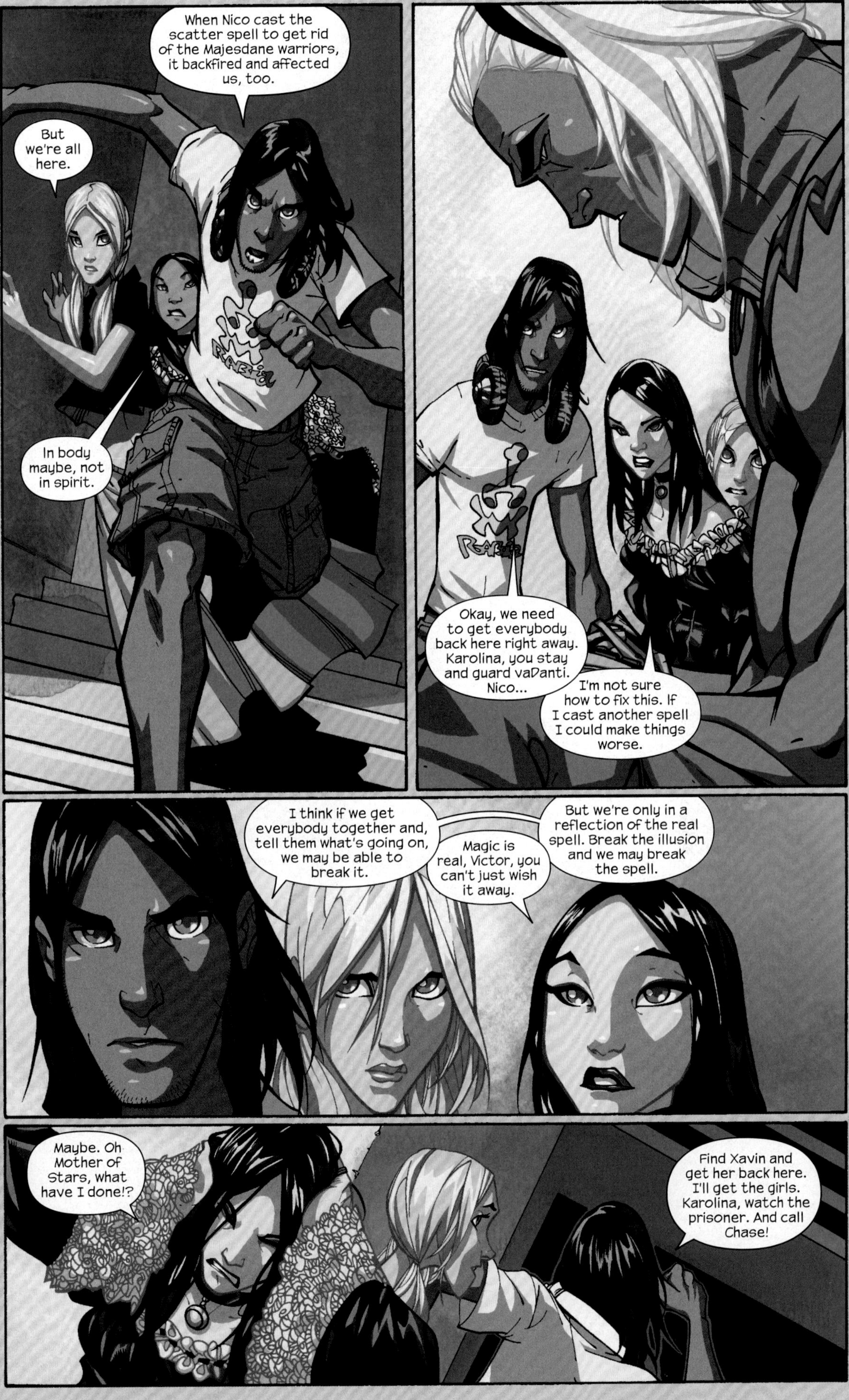
When Nico cast the scatter spell to get rid of the Majesdane warriors, it backfired and affected us, too.
But we're all here.
In body maybe, not in spirit.
Okay, we need to get everybody back here right away. Karolina, you stay and guard vaDanti. Nico...
I'm not sure how to fix this. If I cast another spell I could make things worse.
I think if we get everybody together and, tell them what's going on, we may be able to break it.
Magic is real, Victor, you can't just wish it away.
But we're only in a reflection of the real spell. Break the illusion and we may break the spell.
Maybe. Oh Mother of Stars, what have I done!?
Find Xavin and get her back here. I'll get the girls. Karolina, watch the prisoner. And call Chase!

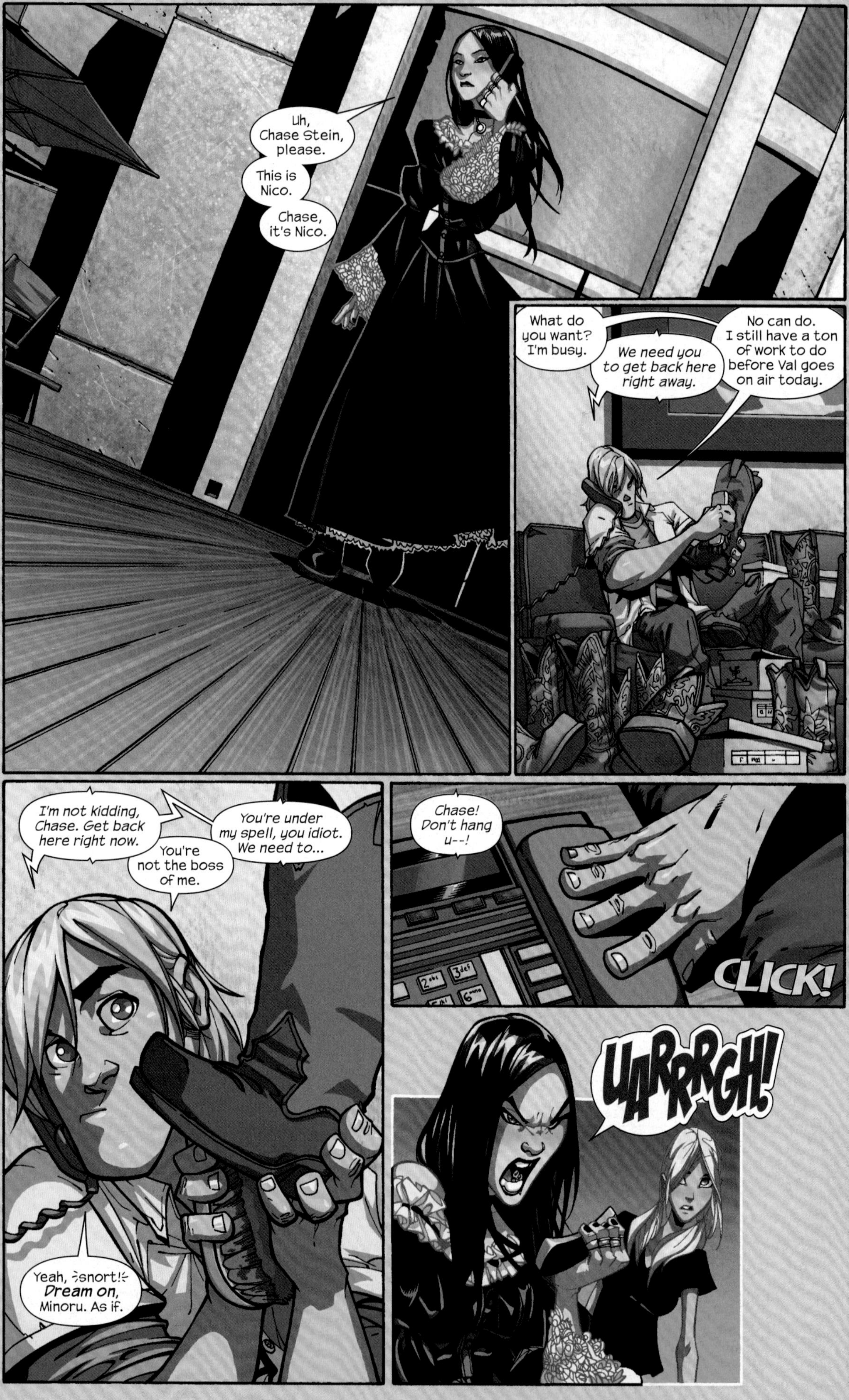
Uh, Chase Stein, please.
This is Nico.
Chase, it's Nico.
What do you want? I'm busy.
We need you to get back here right away.
No can do. I still have a ton of work to do before Val goes on air today.
I'm not kidding, Chase. Get back here right now.
You're not the boss of me.
You're under my spell, you idiot. We need to...
Yeah, *snort!* *Dream on*, Minoru. As if.
Chase! Don't hang u--!
CLICK!
UARRRGH!

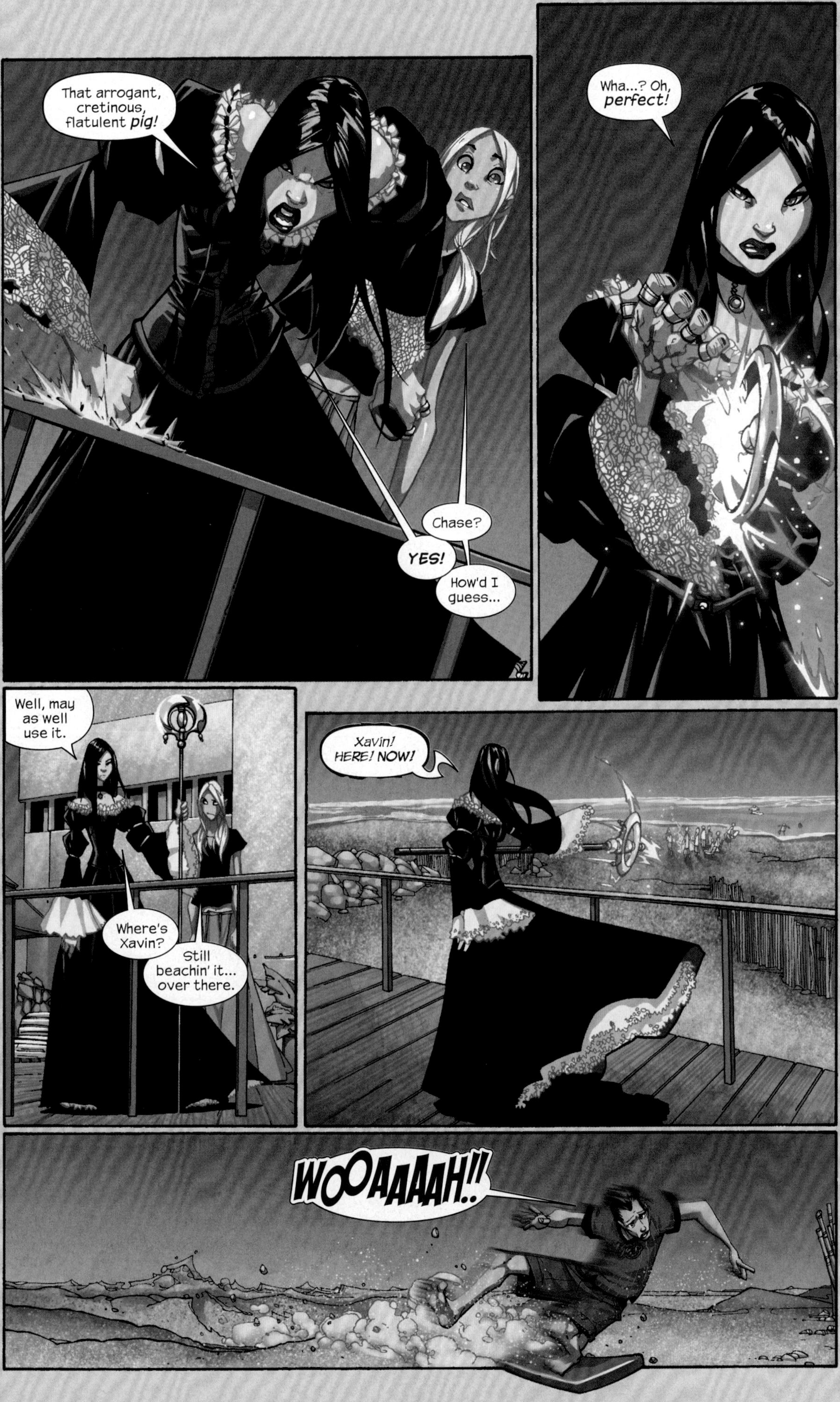
That arrogant, cretinous, flatulent *pig!*
Chase?
*YES!*
How'd I guess...
Wha...? Oh, *perfect!*
Well, may as well use it.
Where's Xavin?
Still beachin' it... over there.
*Xavin! HERE! NOW!*
WOOAAAAH!!

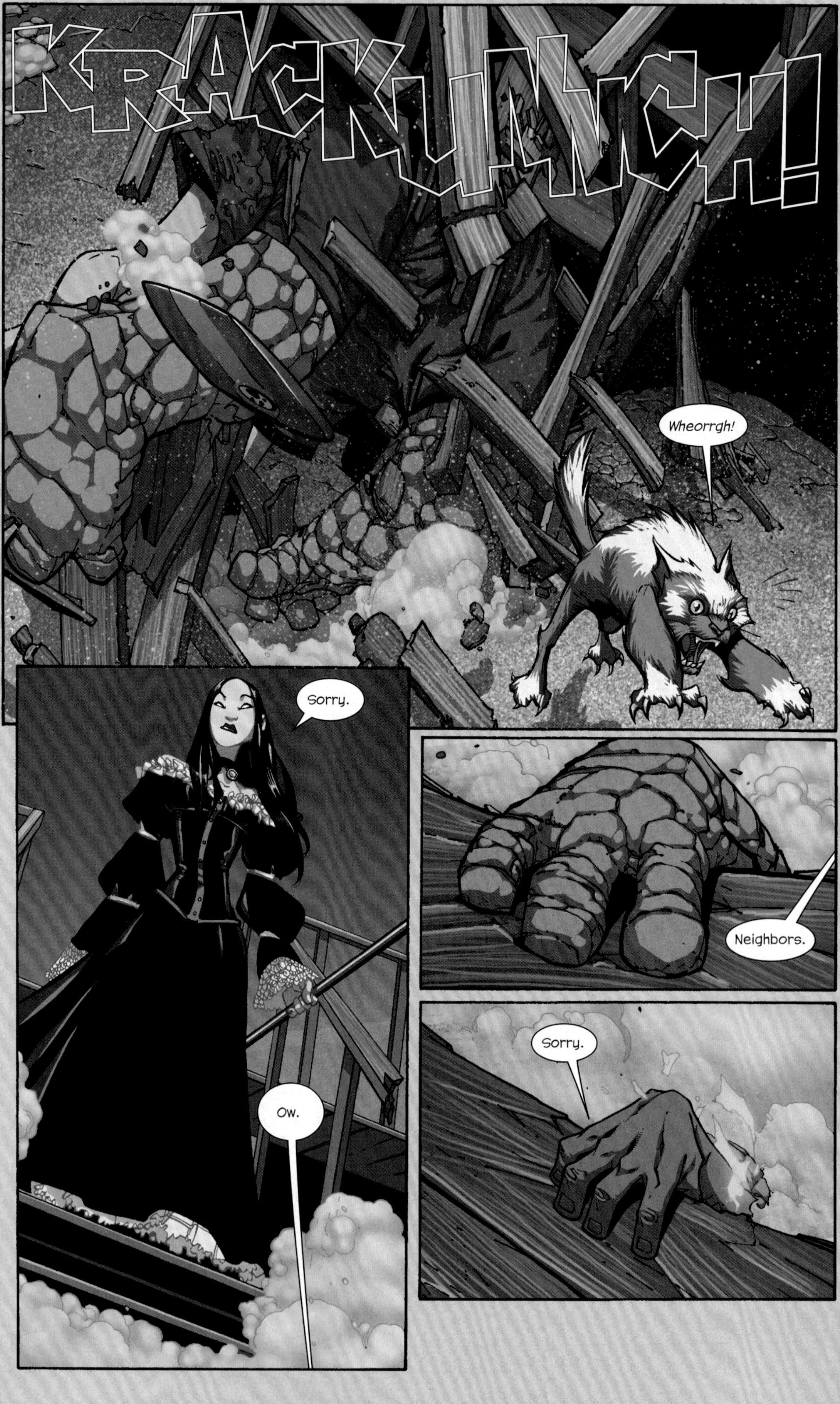
KRACKUMMCH!
Wheorrgh!
Sorry.
Ow.
Neighbors.
Sorry.

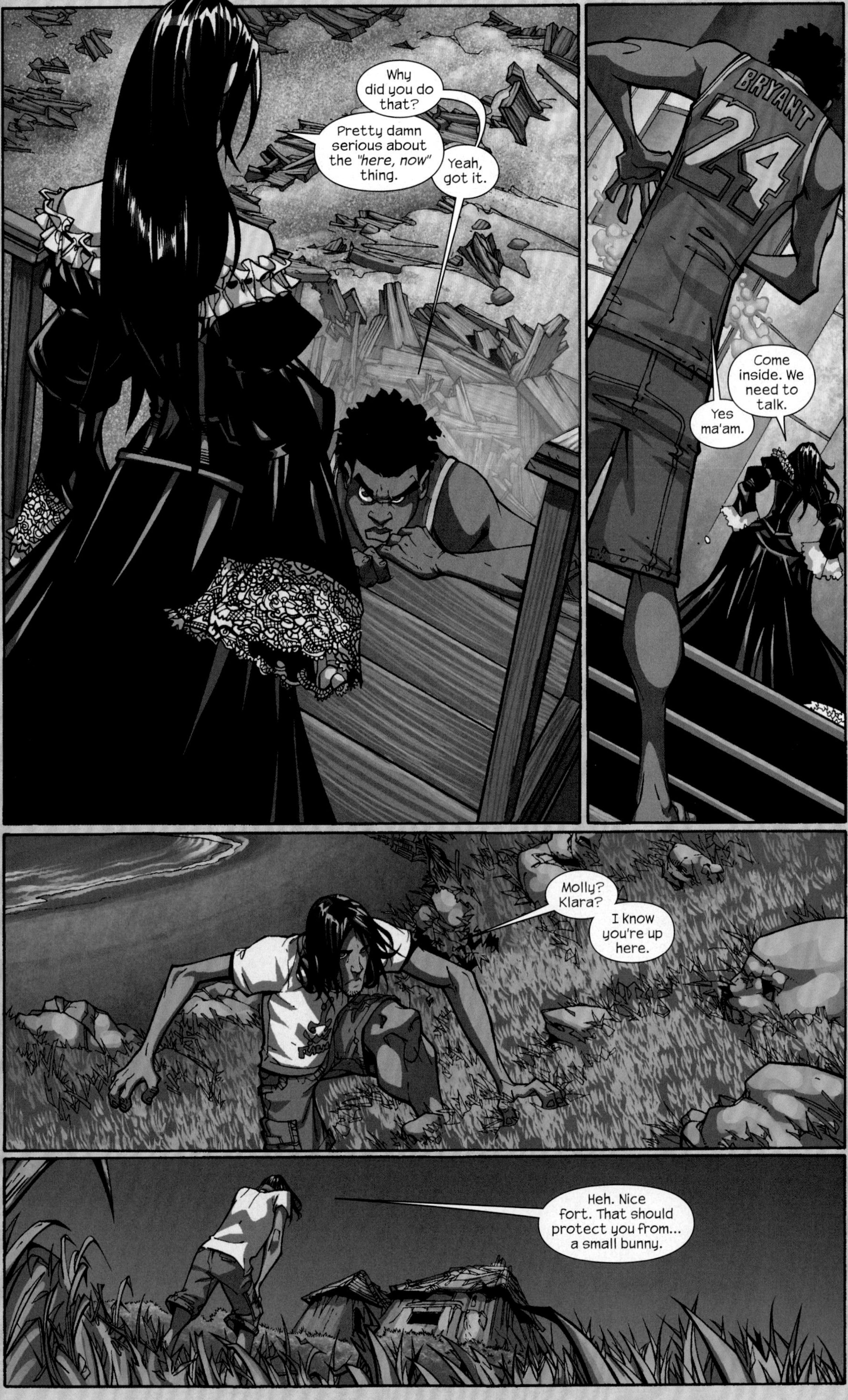

Why did you do that?
Pretty damn serious about the "here, now" thing.
Yeah, got it.
BRYANT 24
Come inside. We need to talk.
Yes ma'am.
Molly? Klara?
I know you're up here.
Heh. Nice fort. That should protect you from... a small bunny.

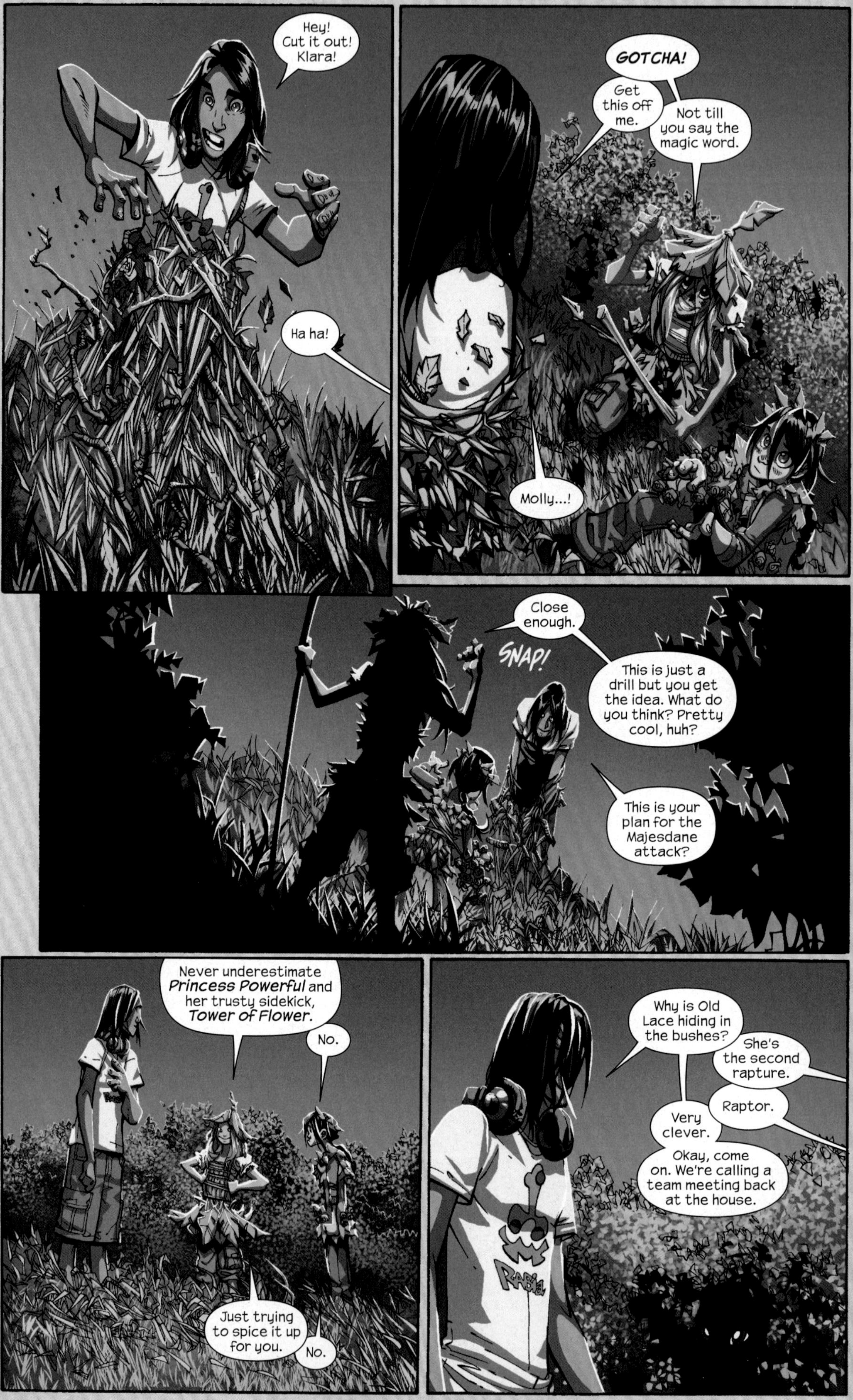
Hey! Cut it out! Klara!
Ha ha!
GOTCHA!
Get this off me.
Not till you say the magic word.
Molly...!
Close enough.
SNAP!
This is just a drill but you get the idea. What do you think? Pretty cool, huh?
This is your plan for the Majesdane attack?
Never underestimate Princess Powerful and her trusty sidekick, Tower of Flower.
No.
Just trying to spice it up for you.
No.
Why is Old Lace hiding in the bushes?
She's the second rapture.
Raptor.
Very clever.
Okay, come on. We're calling a team meeting back at the house.

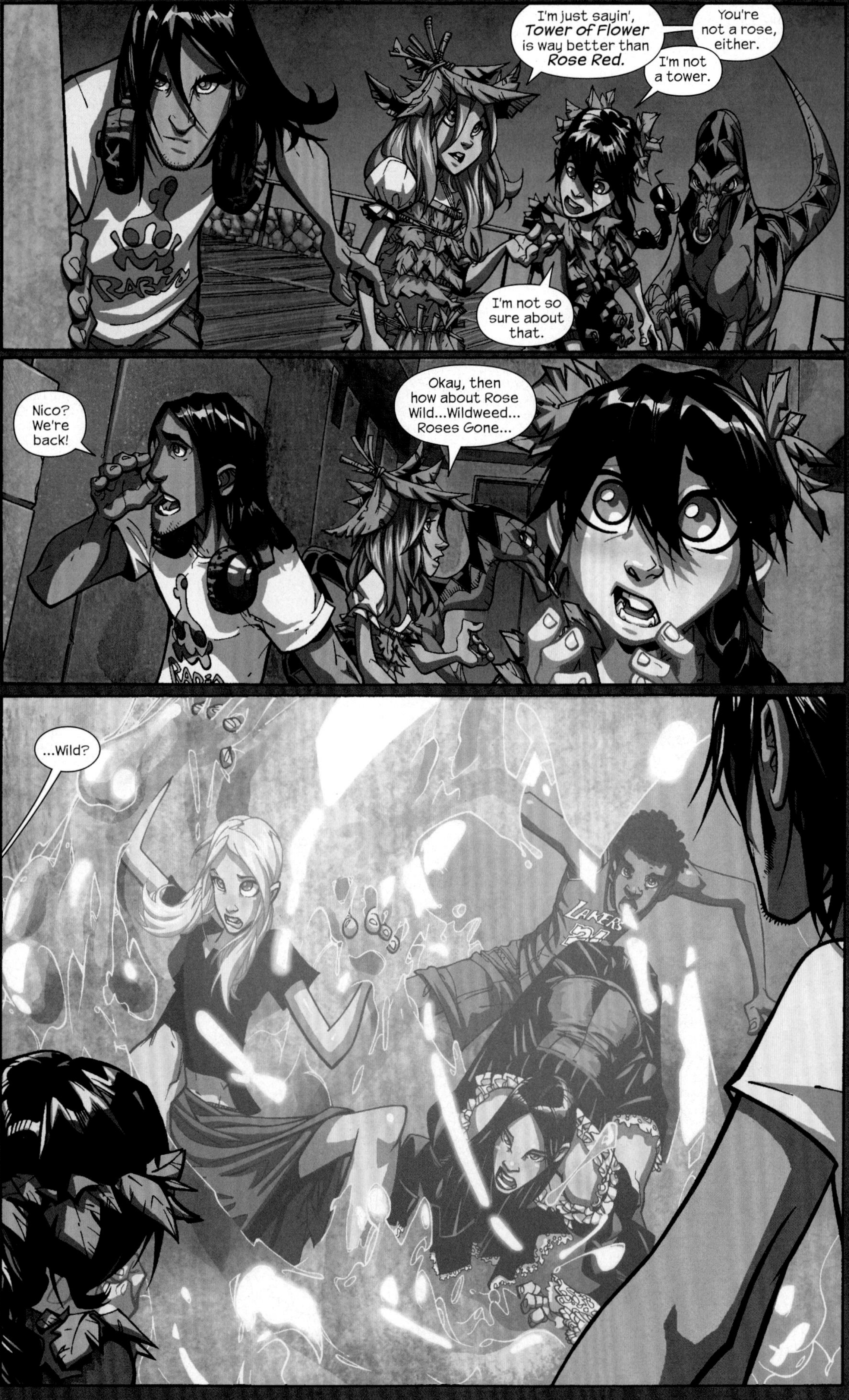
I'm just sayin', Tower of Flower is way better than Rose Red.
You're not a rose, either.
I'm not a tower.
I'm not so sure about that.
Nico? We're back!
Okay, then how about Rose Wild...Wildweed... Roses Gone...
...Wild?
RABIA
LAKERS

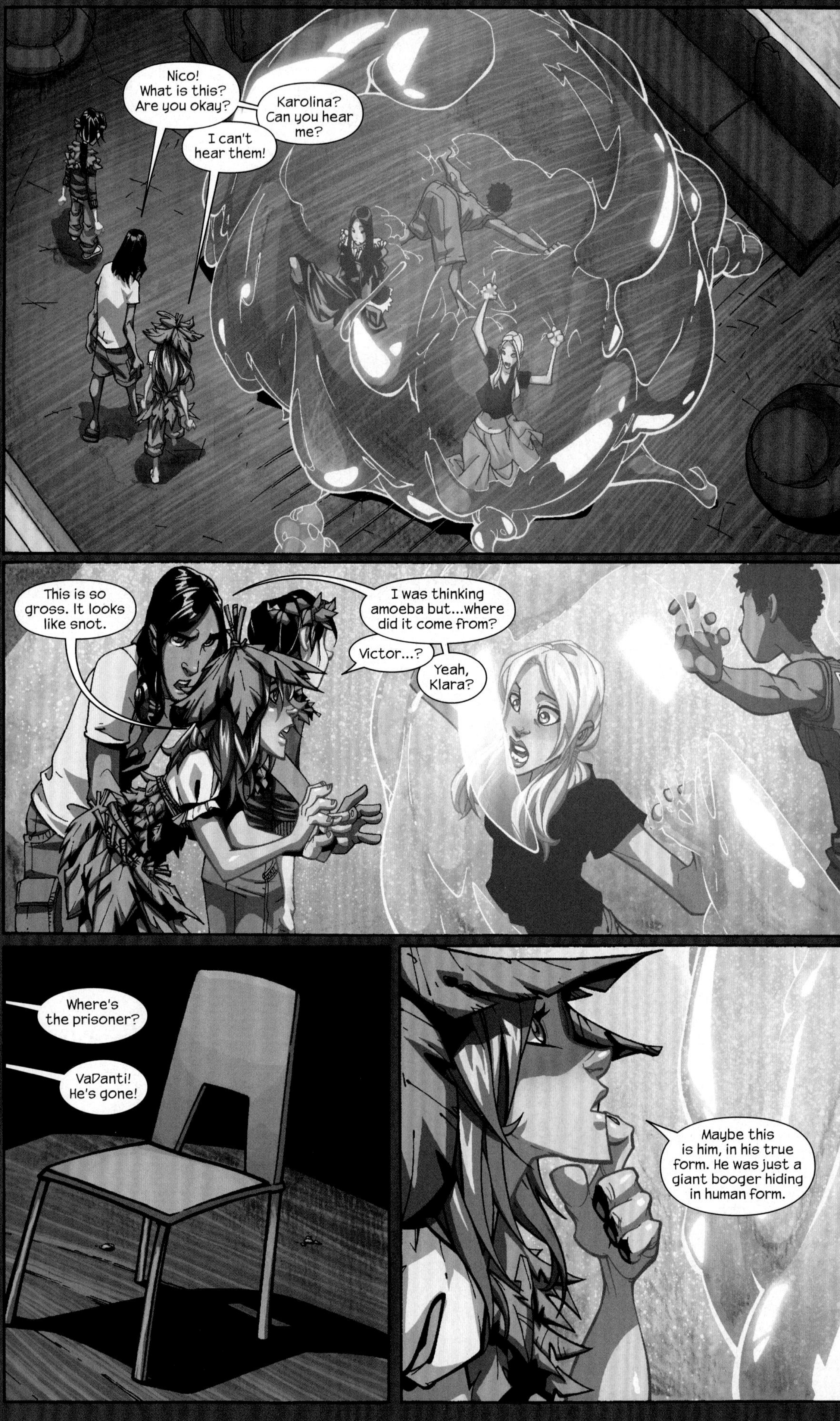
Nico!
What is this?
Are you okay?
Karolina?
Can you hear
me?
I can't
hear them!
This is so
gross. It looks
like snot.
I was thinking
amoeba but...where
did it come from?
Victor...?
Yeah,
Klara?
Where's
the prisoner?
VaDanti!
He's gone!
Maybe this
is him, in his true
form. He was just a
giant booger hiding
in human form.

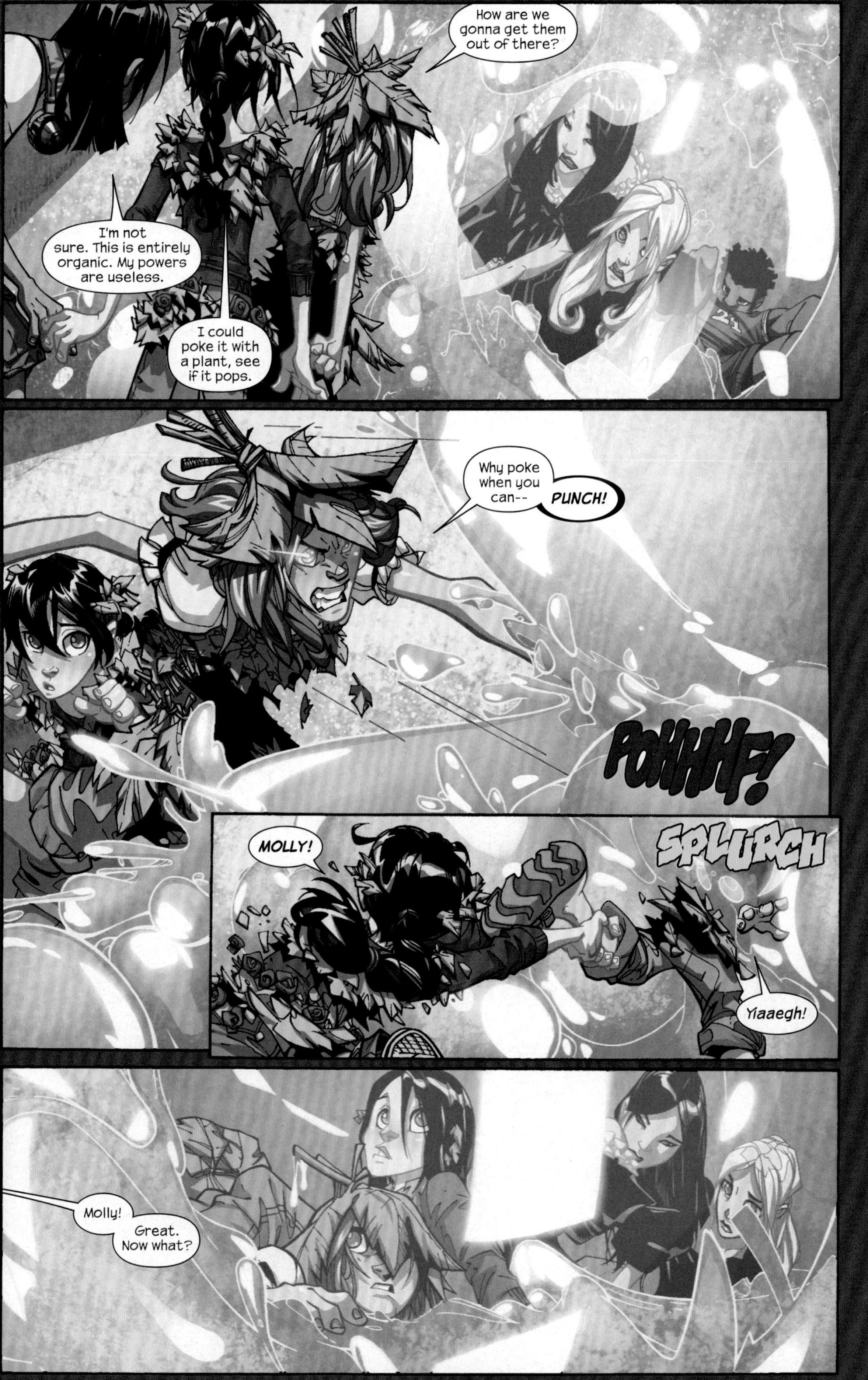
How are we gonna get them out of there?
I'm not sure. This is entirely organic. My powers are useless.
I could poke it with a plant, see if it pops.
Why poke when you can--
PUNCH!
POHHHF!
MOLLY!
SPLURCH
Yiaaegh!
Molly!
Great. Now what?

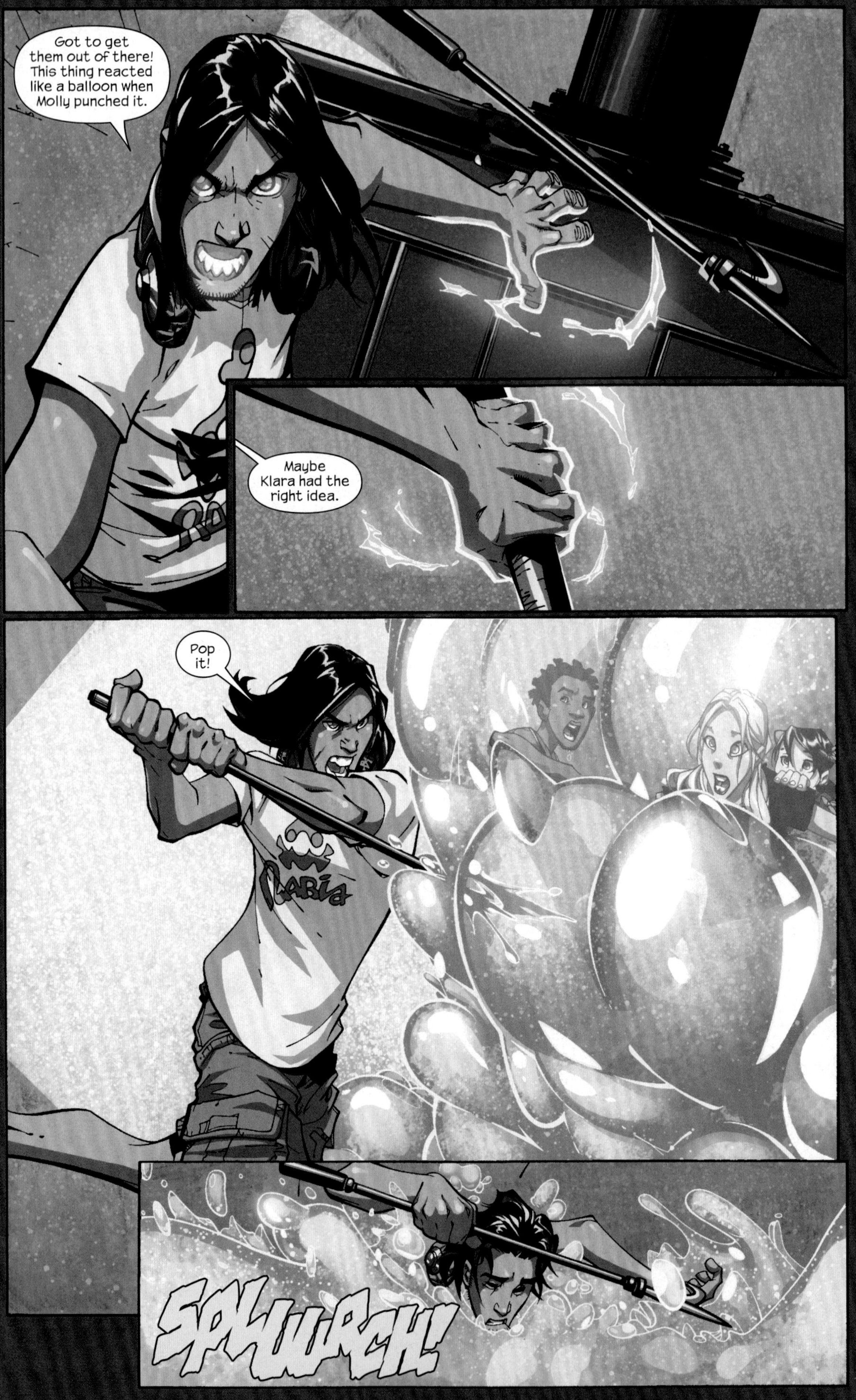
Got to get them out of there! This thing reacted like a balloon when Molly punched it.
Maybe Klara had the right idea.
Pop it!
SPLUURCH!

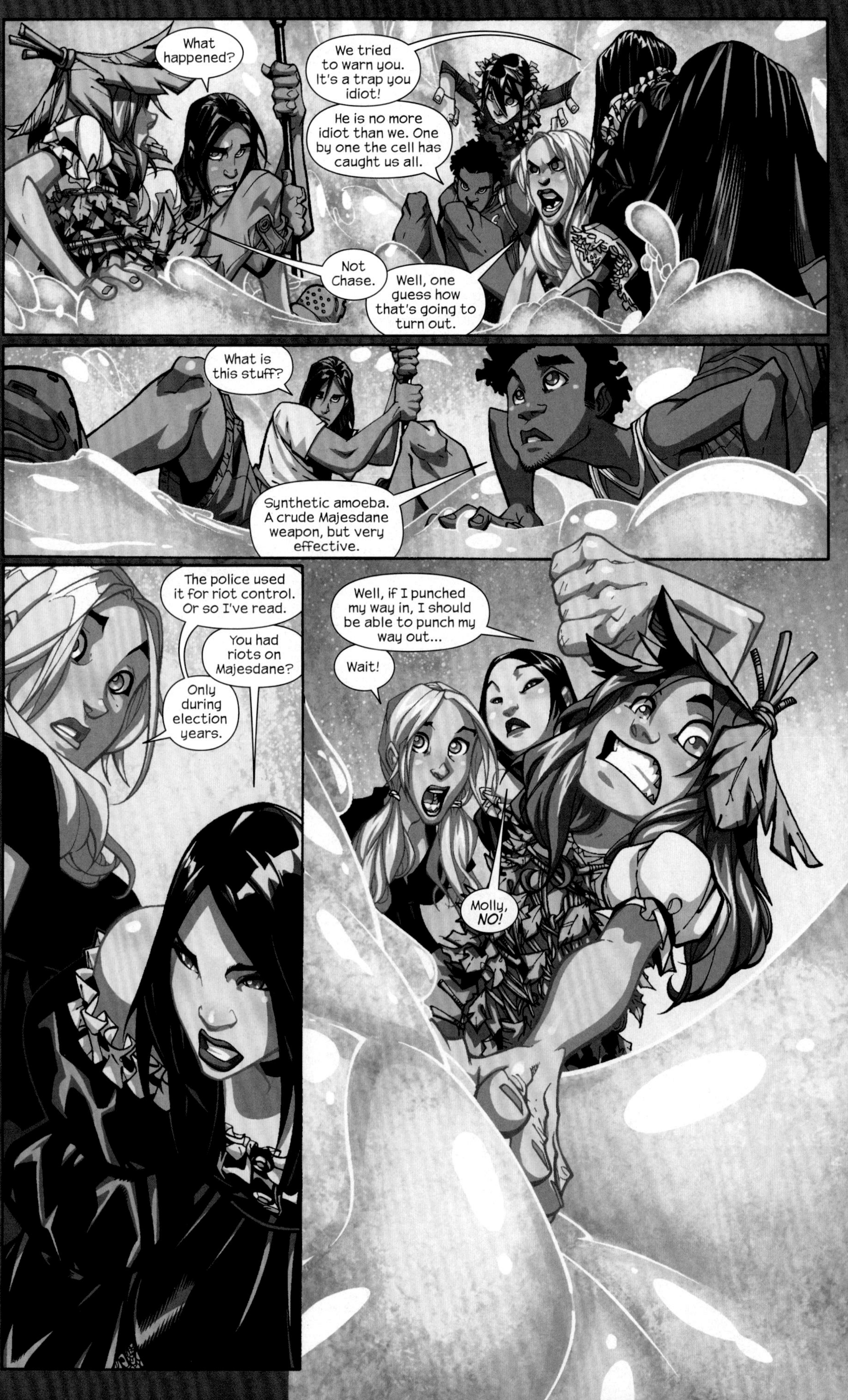
What happened?
We tried to warn you. It's a trap you idiot!
He is no more idiot than we. One by one the cell has caught us all.
Not Chase.
Well, one guess how that's going to turn out.
What is this stuff?
Synthetic amoeba. A crude Majesdane weapon, but very effective.
The police used it for riot control. Or so I've read.
You had riots on Majesdane?
Only during election years.
Well, if I punched my way in, I should be able to punch my way out...
Wait!
Molly, NO!

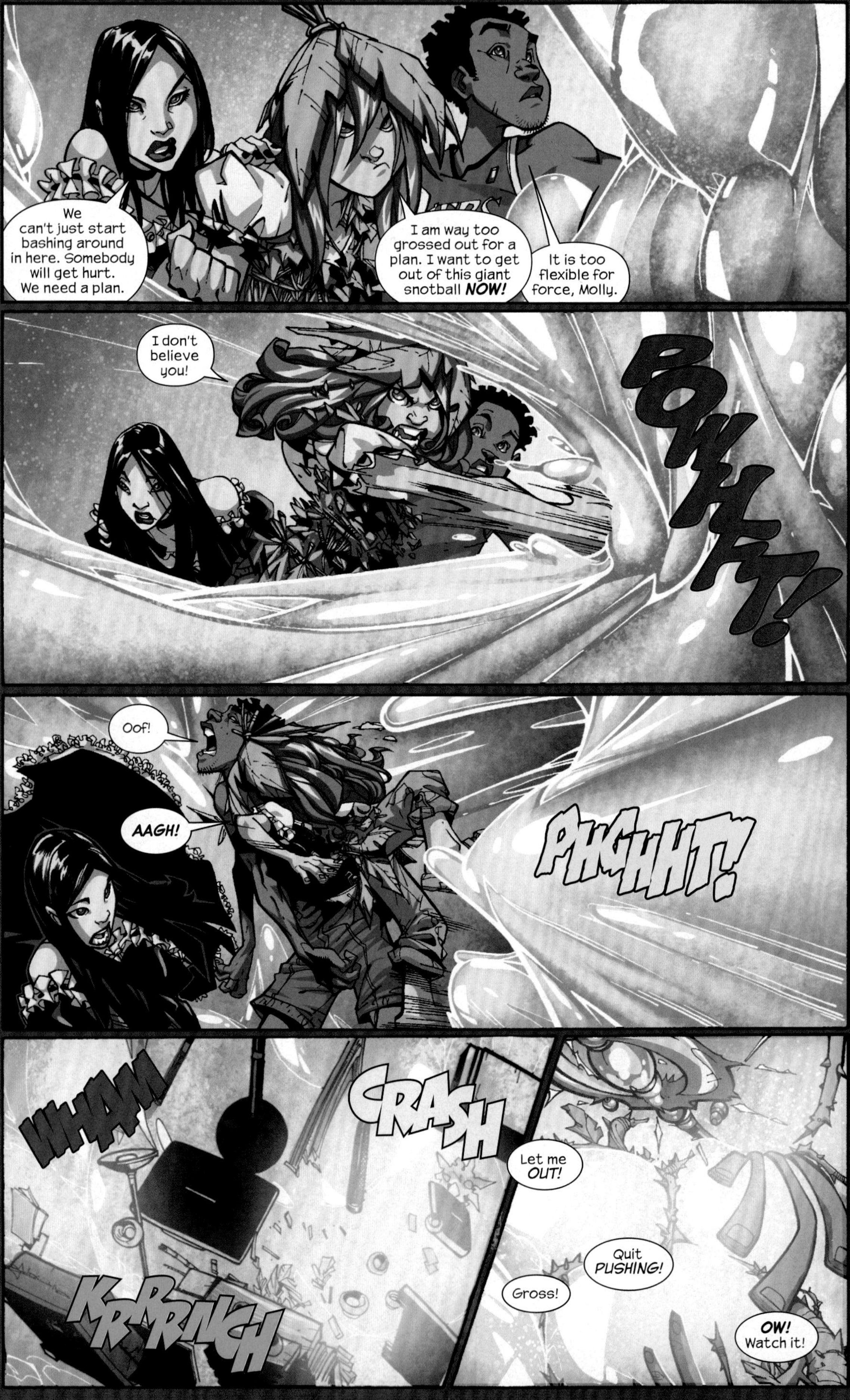
We can't just start bashing around in here. Somebody will get hurt. We need a plan.
I am way too grossed out for a plan. I want to get out of this giant snotball **NOW!**
It is too flexible for force, Molly.
I don't believe you!
POWHFT!
Oof!
AAGH!
PHGHHT!
WHAM
CRASH
KRRRNCH
Let me *OUT!*
Quit *PUSHING!*
Gross!
**OW!** Watch it!

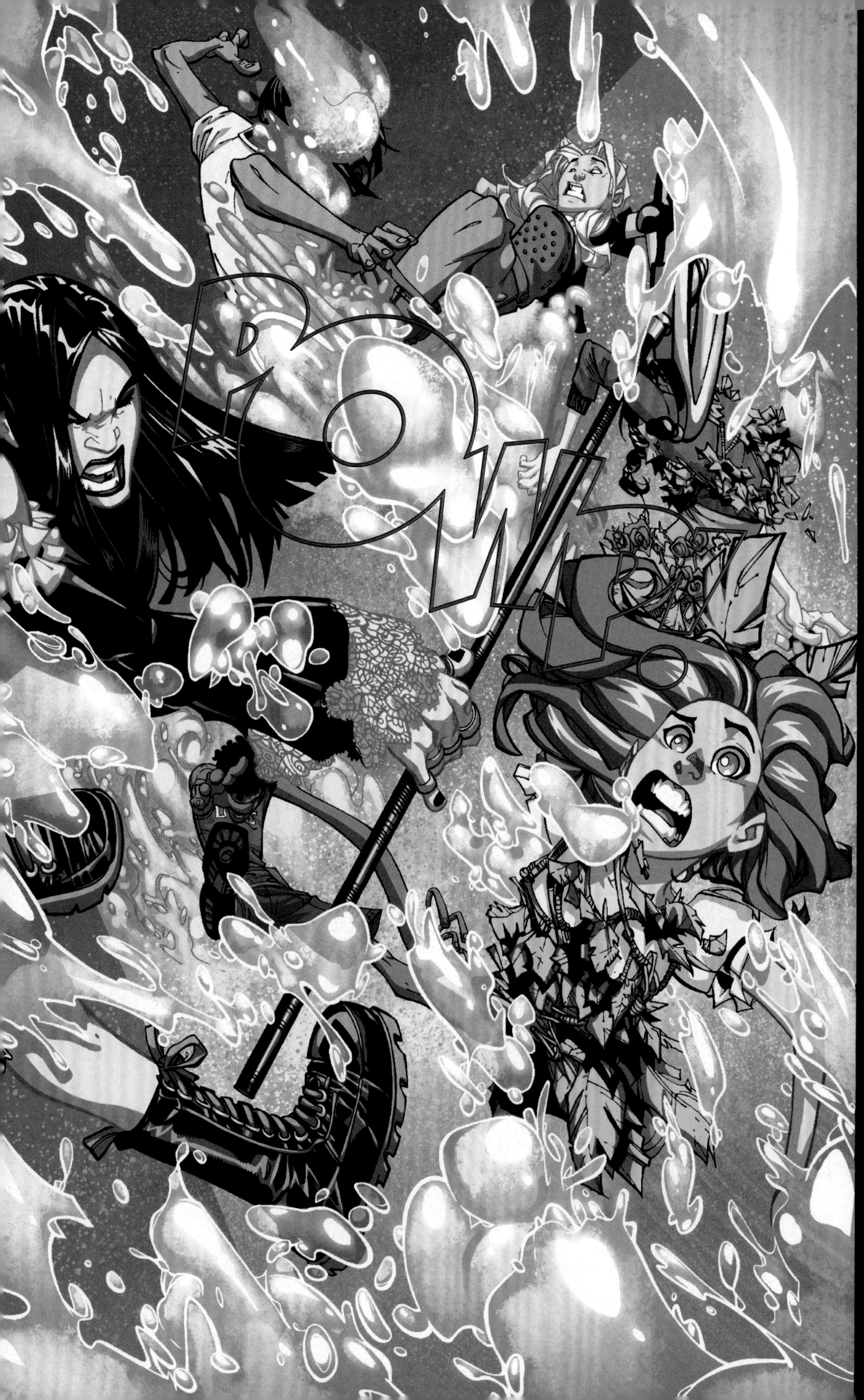

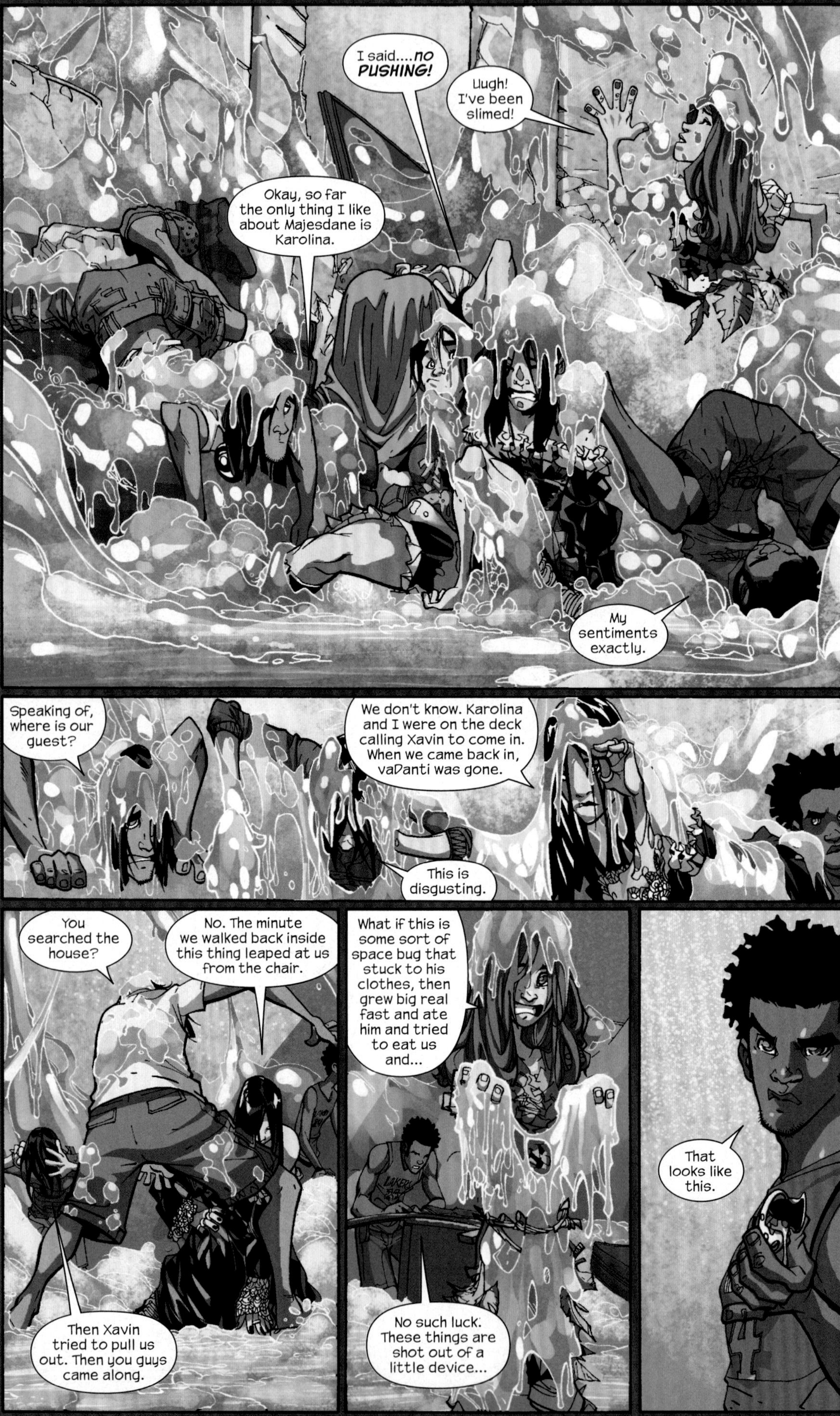
I said....NO PUSHING!
Uugh! I've been slimed!
Okay, so far the only thing I like about Majesdane is Karolina.
My sentiments exactly.
Speaking of, where is our guest?
We don't know. Karolina and I were on the deck calling Xavin to come in. When we came back in, vaDanti was gone.
This is disgusting.
You searched the house?
No. The minute we walked back inside this thing leaped at us from the chair.
Then Xavin tried to pull us out. Then you guys came along.
What if this is some sort of space bug that stuck to his clothes, then grew big real fast and ate him and tried to eat us and...
No such luck. These things are shot out of a little device...
That looks like this.

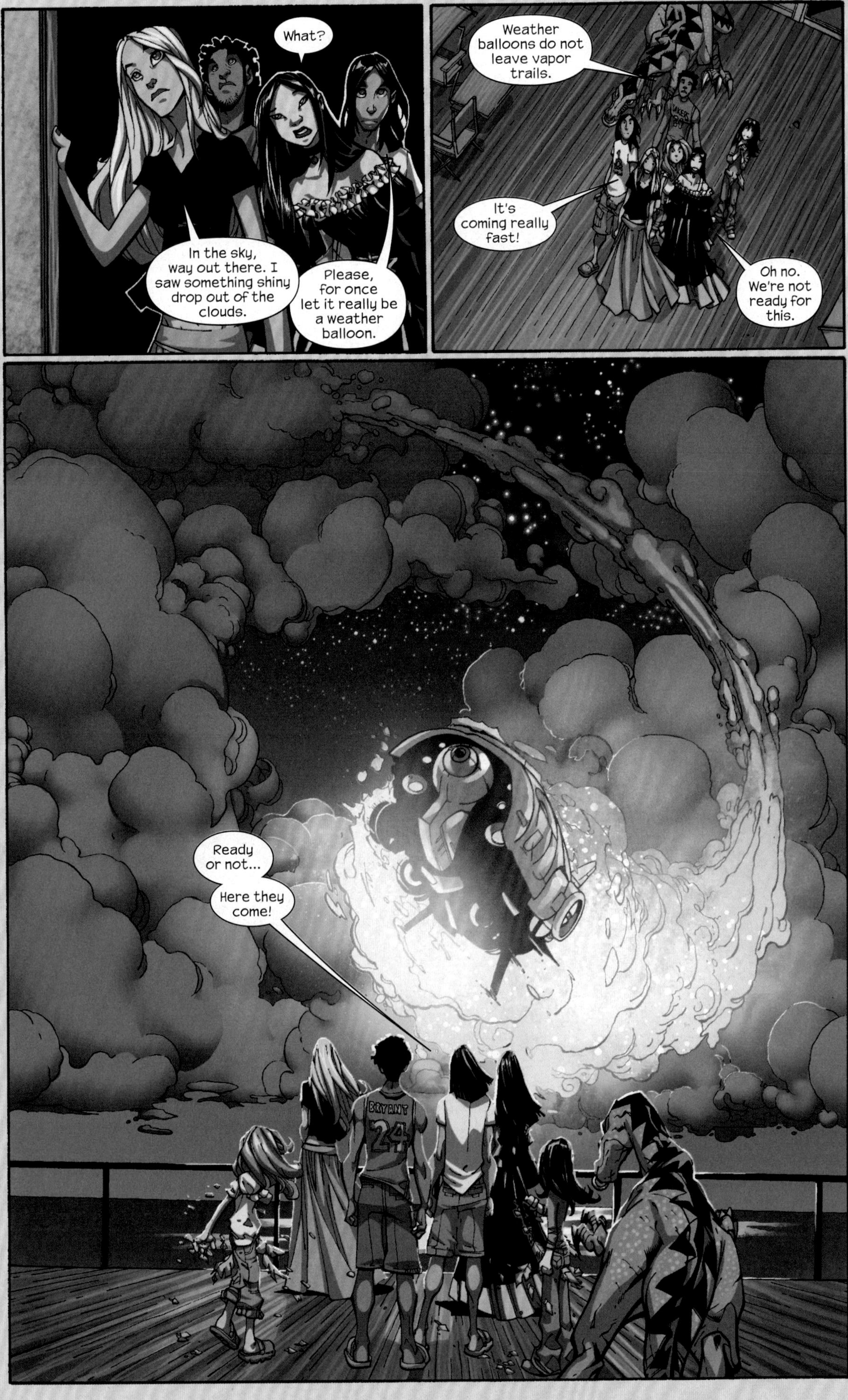
What?
In the sky, way out there. I saw something shiny drop out of the clouds.
Please, for once let it really be a weather balloon.
Weather balloons do not leave vapor trails.
It's coming really fast!
Oh no. We're not ready for this.
Ready or not...
Here they come!
BRYANT
24

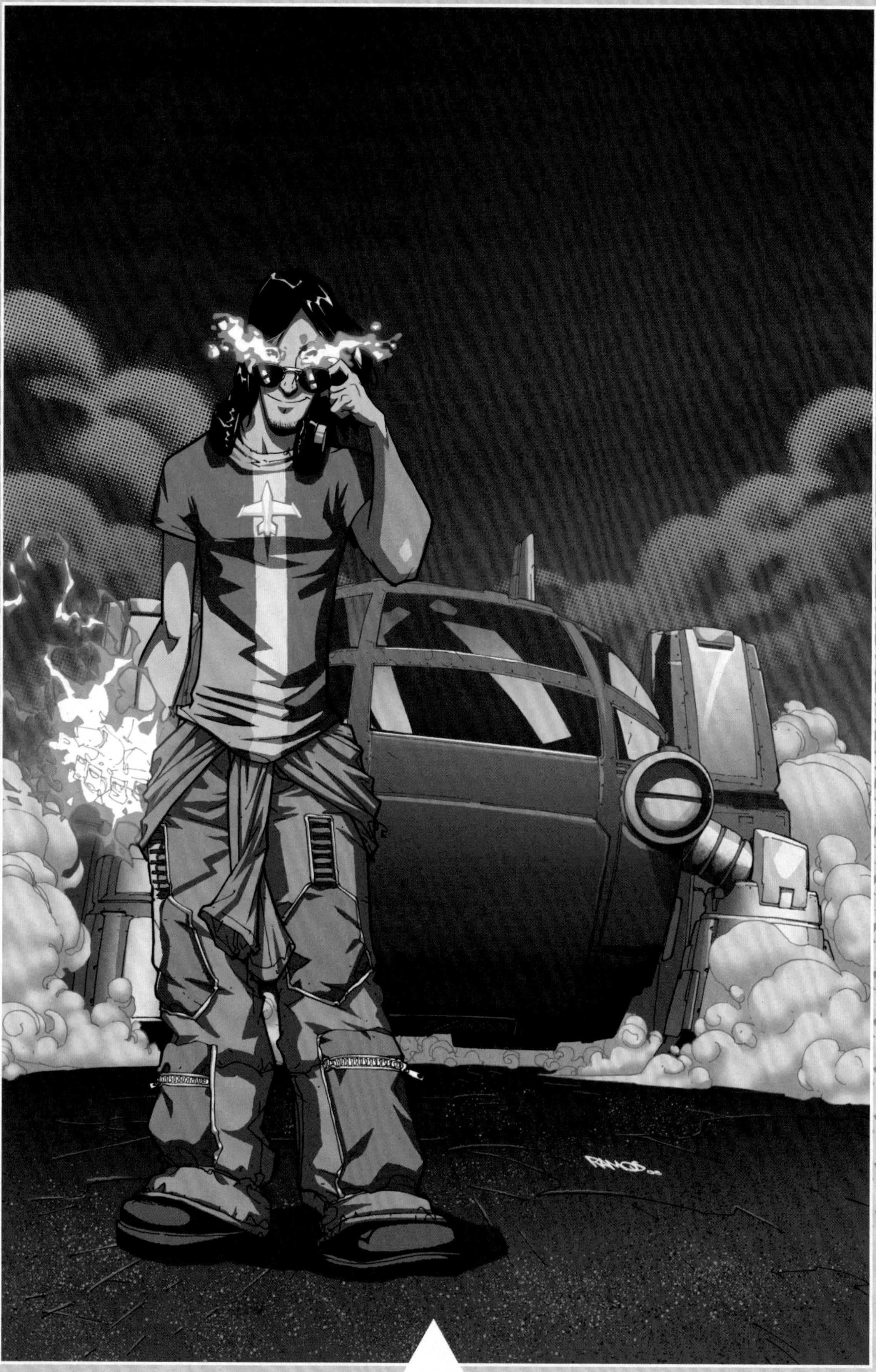

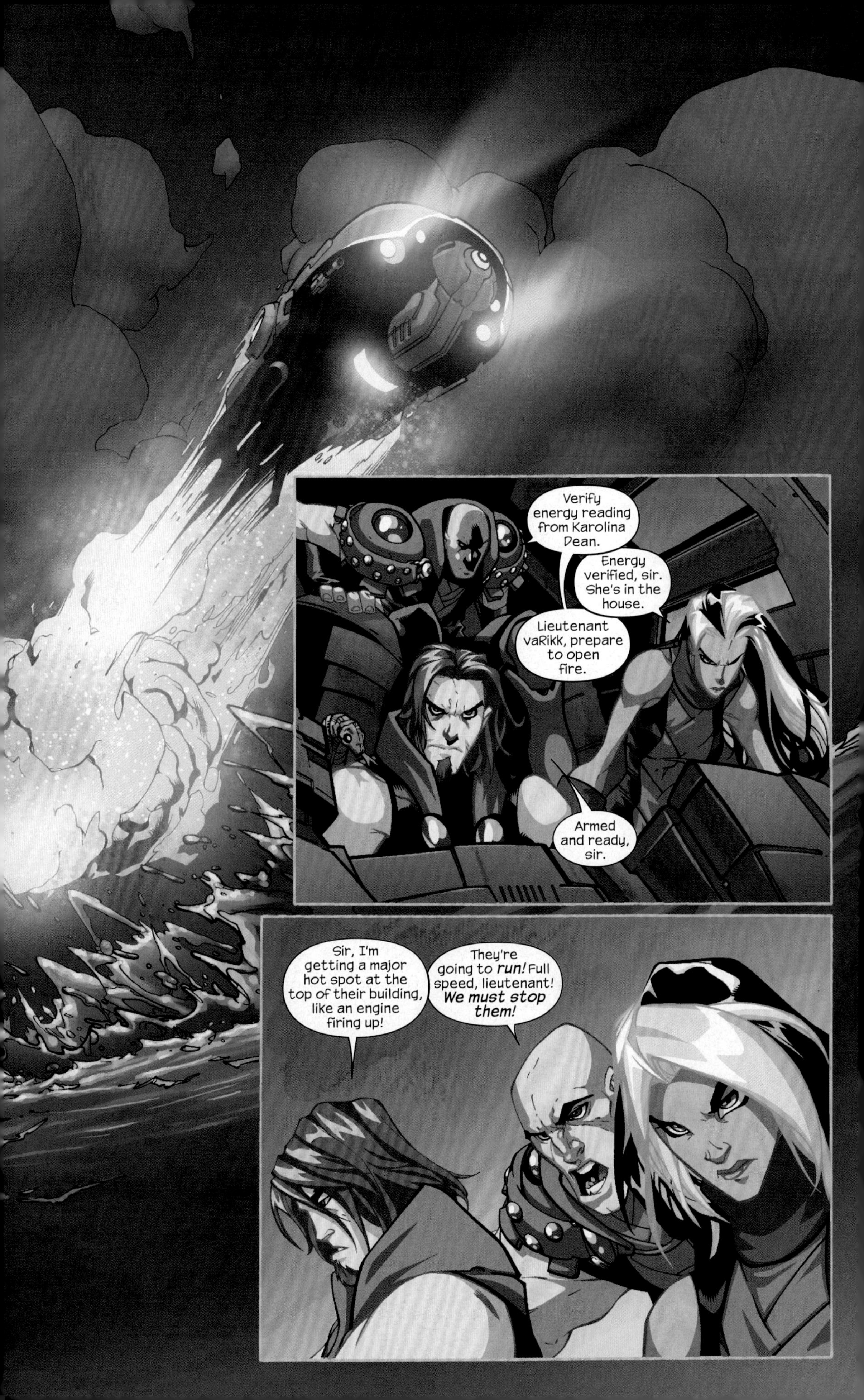
Verify energy reading from Karolina Dean.
Energy verified, sir. She's in the house.
Lieutenant vaRikk, prepare to open fire.
Armed and ready, sir.
Sir, I'm getting a major hot spot at the top of their building, like an engine firing up!
They're going to *run!* Full speed, lieutenant! ***We must stop them!***

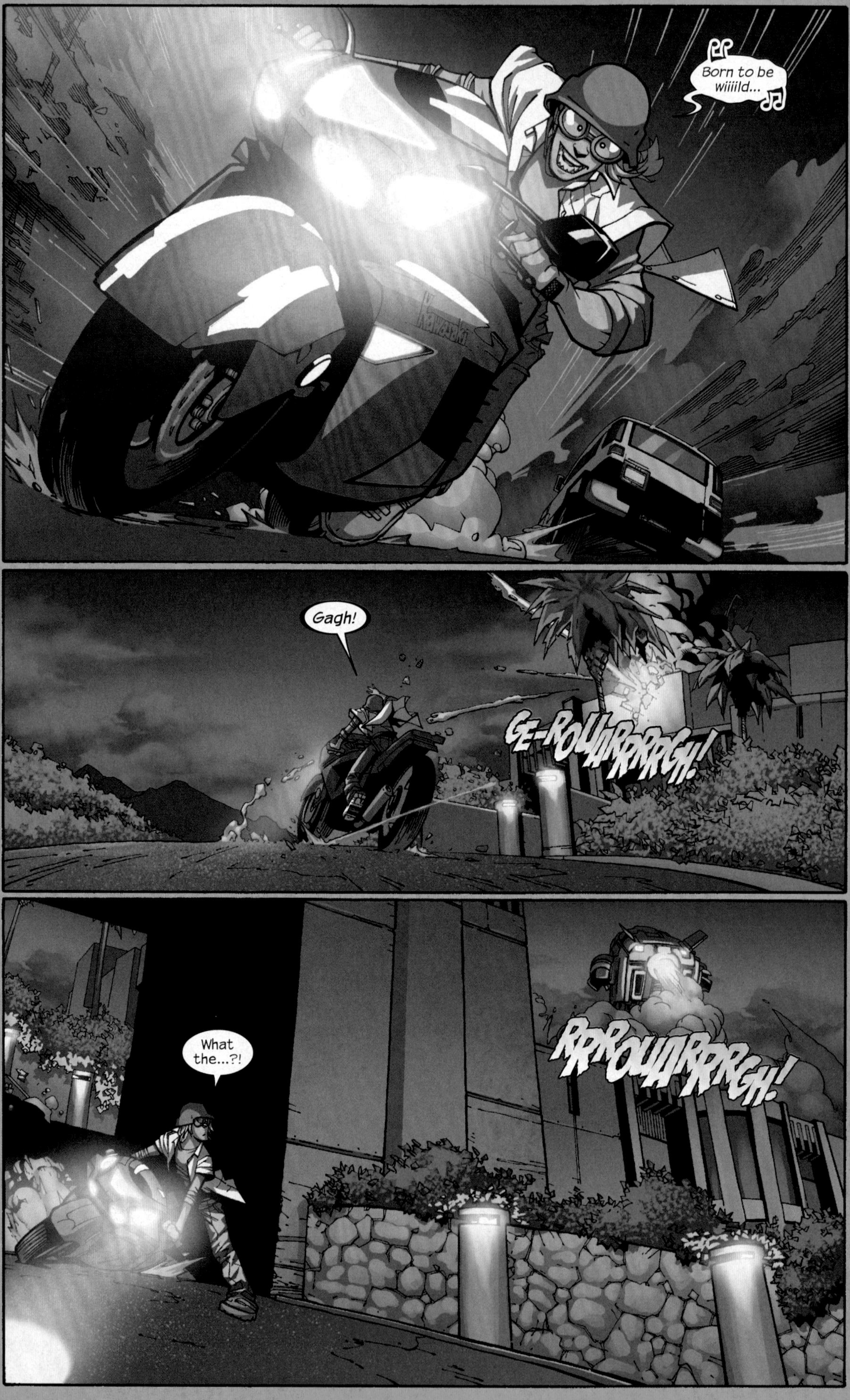
Born to be wiiiild...
Gagh!
GE-ROUARRRRGH!
What the...?!
RRROUARRRGH!

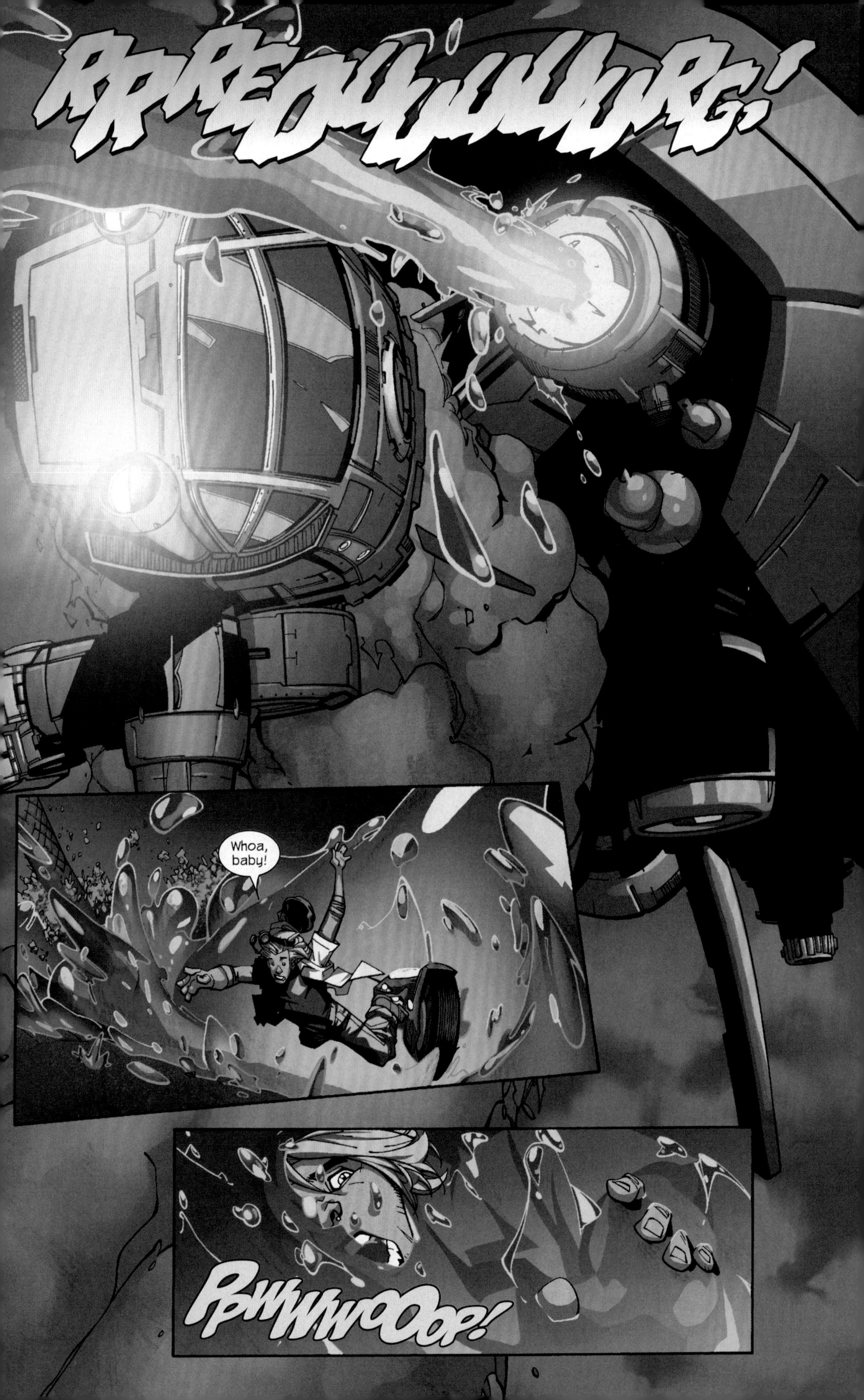
RRREOWWWWRG!
Whoa, baby!
PSHWWOOOP!

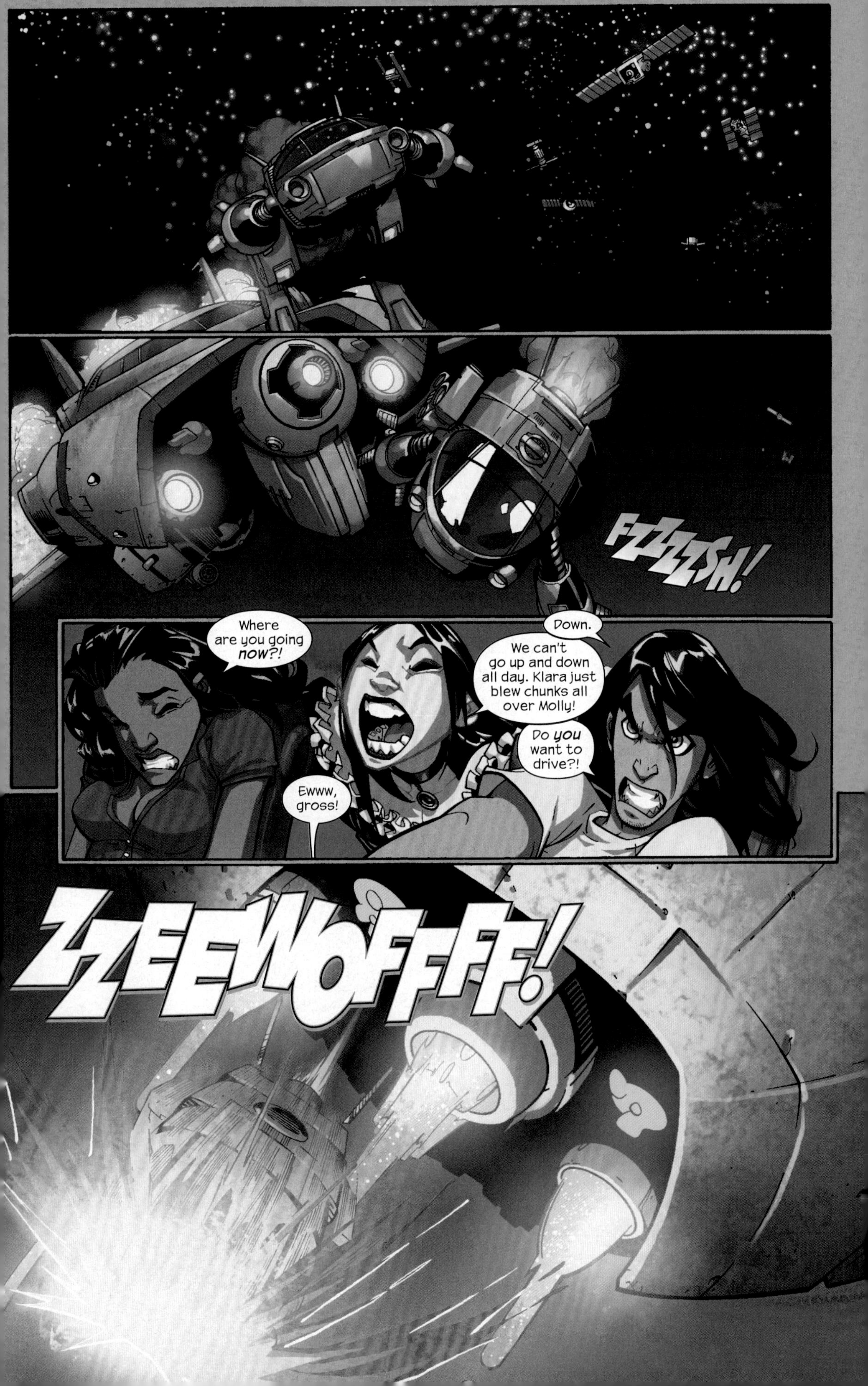
FZZZZSH!
Where are you going now?!
Down.
We can't go up and down all day. Klara just blew chunks all over Molly!
Ewww, gross!
Do you want to drive?!
ZZEEWOFFFF!

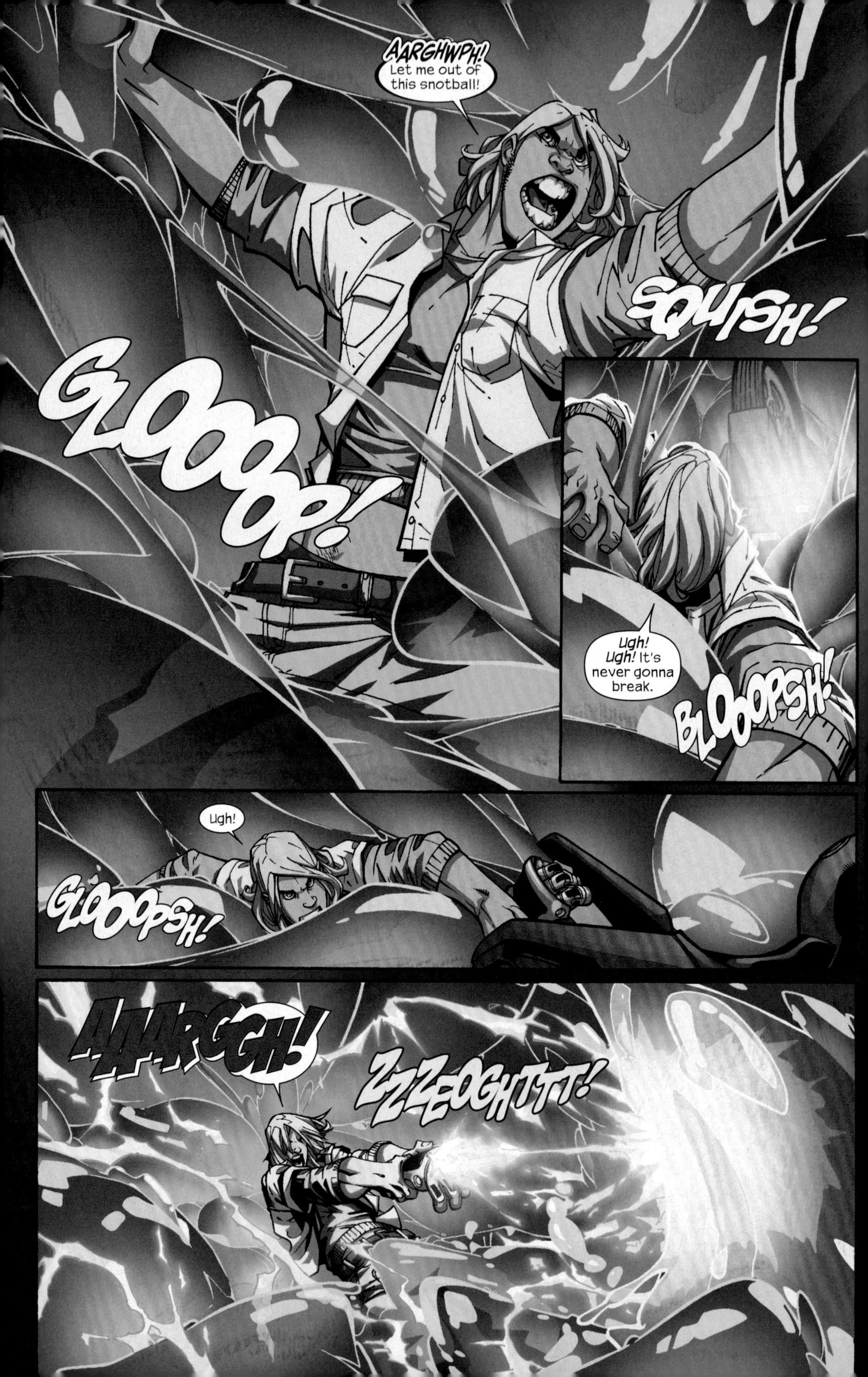
AARGHWPH!
Let me out of this snotball!
SQUISH!
GLOOOOOP!
Ugh! Ugh! It's never gonna break.
BLOOOPSH!
Ugh!
GLOOOPSH!
AAARGGH!
ZZZEOGHTTTT!

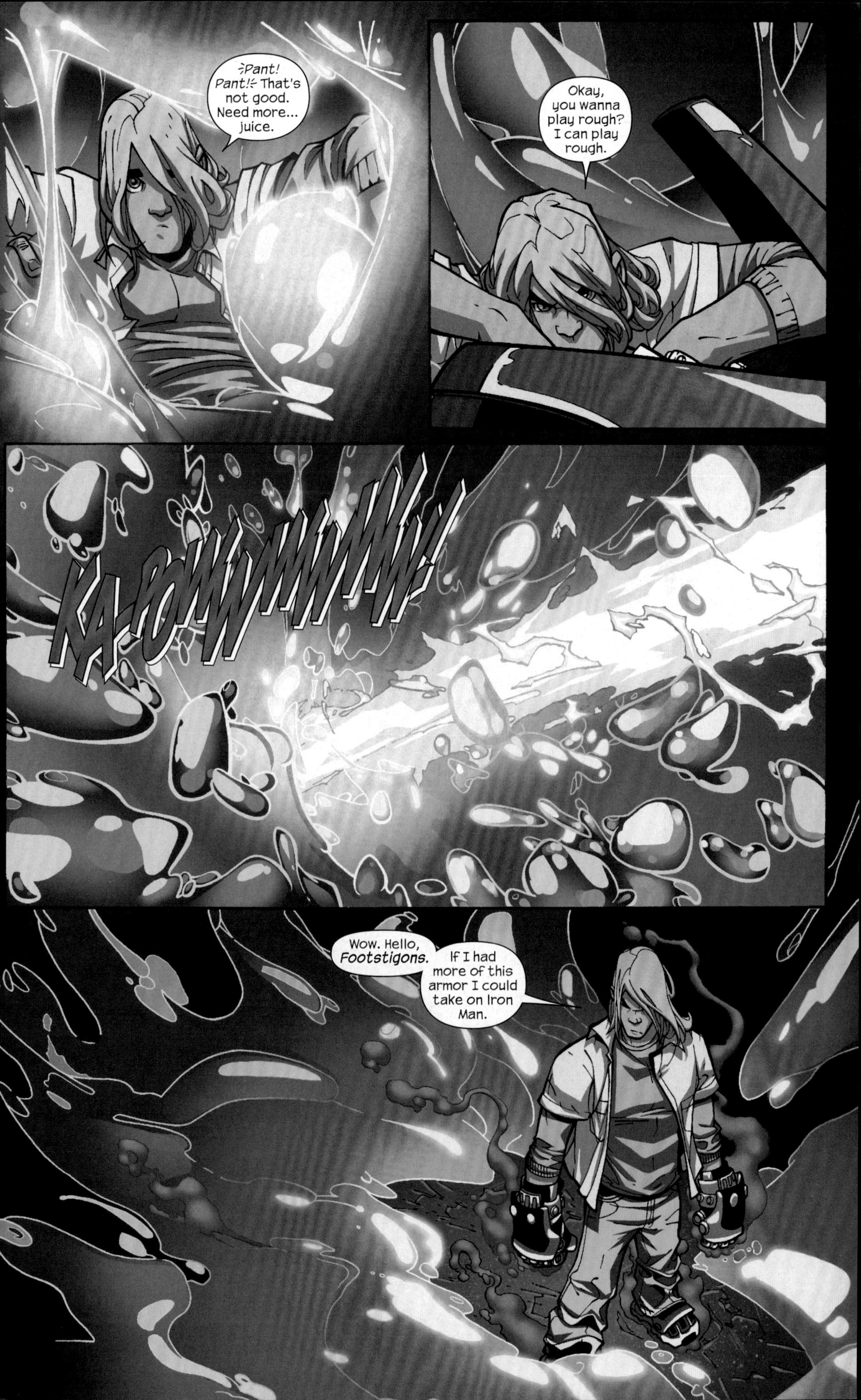

*Pant! Pant!* That's not good. Need more... juice.
Okay, you wanna play rough? I can play rough.
KA-POWWWWWWWW!
Wow. Hello, *Footstigons.*
If I had more of this armor I could take on Iron Man.

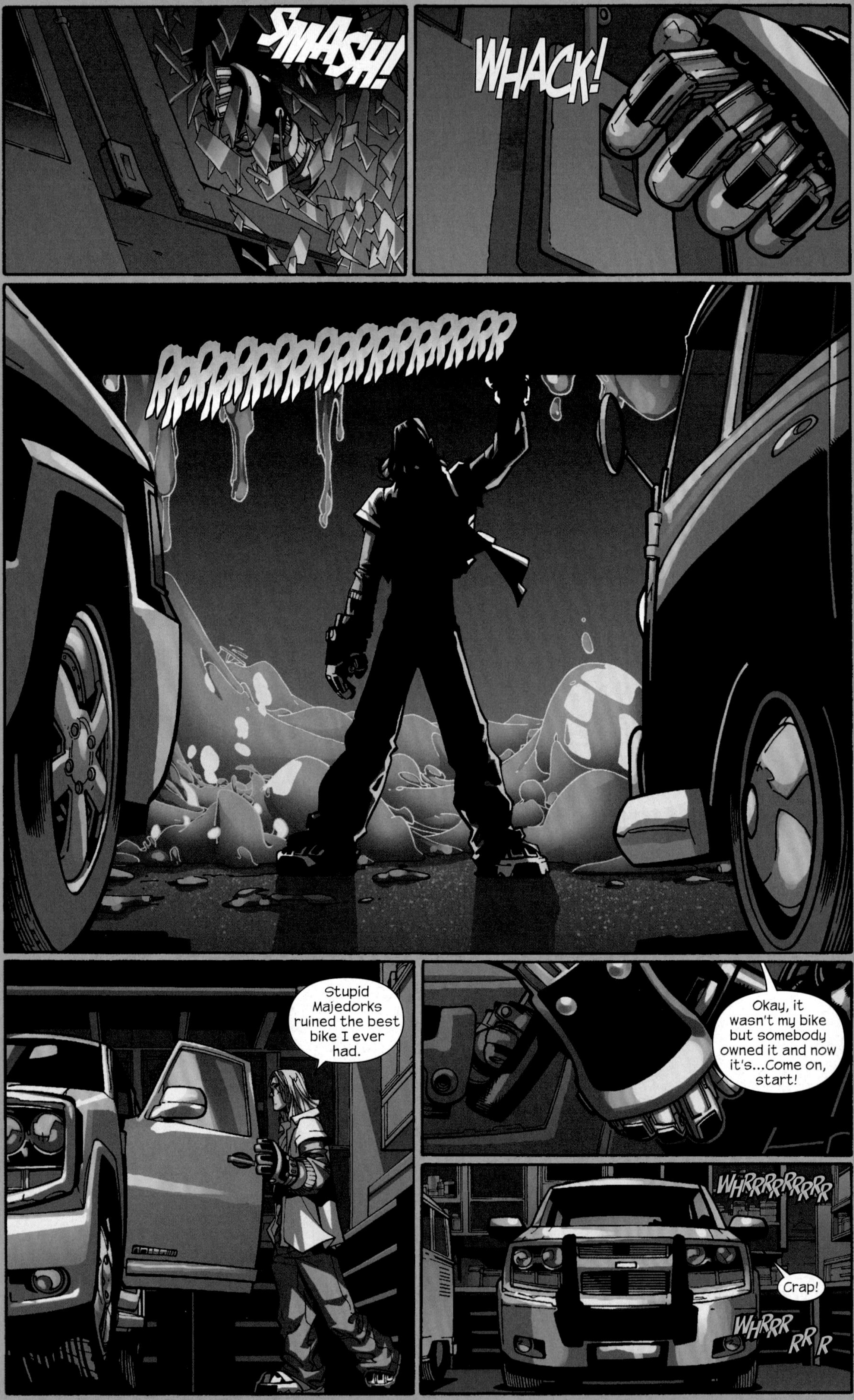
SMASH!
WHACK!
RRRRRRRRRRRRRRRRRRRRRR
Stupid Majedorks ruined the best bike I ever had.
Okay, it wasn't my bike but somebody owned it and now it's...Come on, start!
WHRRRRRRRRR
Crap!
WHRRRRRR

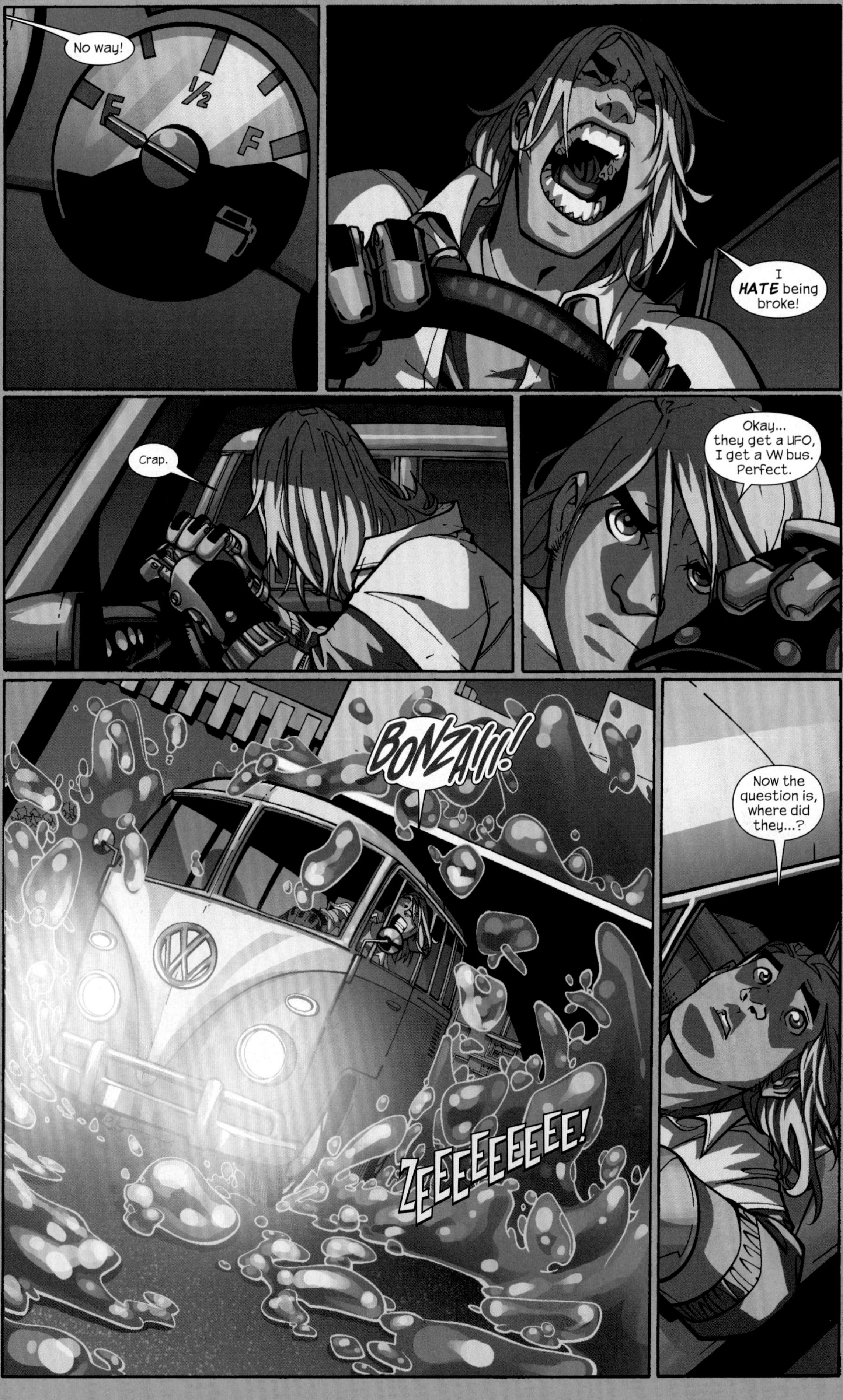

No way!
I HATE being broke!
Crap.
Okay... they get a UFO, I get a VW bus. Perfect.
BONZAAA!
ZEEEEEEEEE!
Now the question is, where did they...?

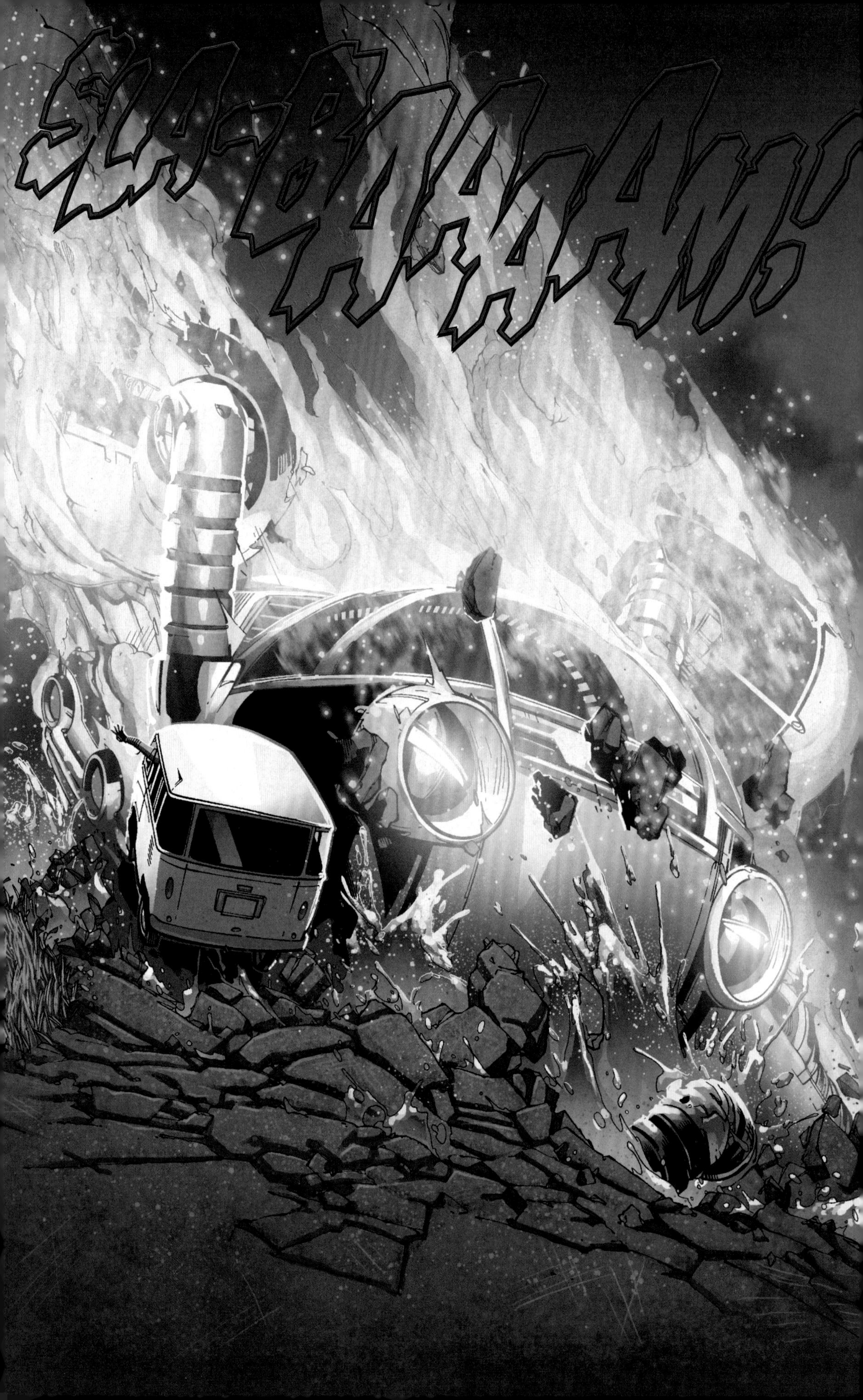

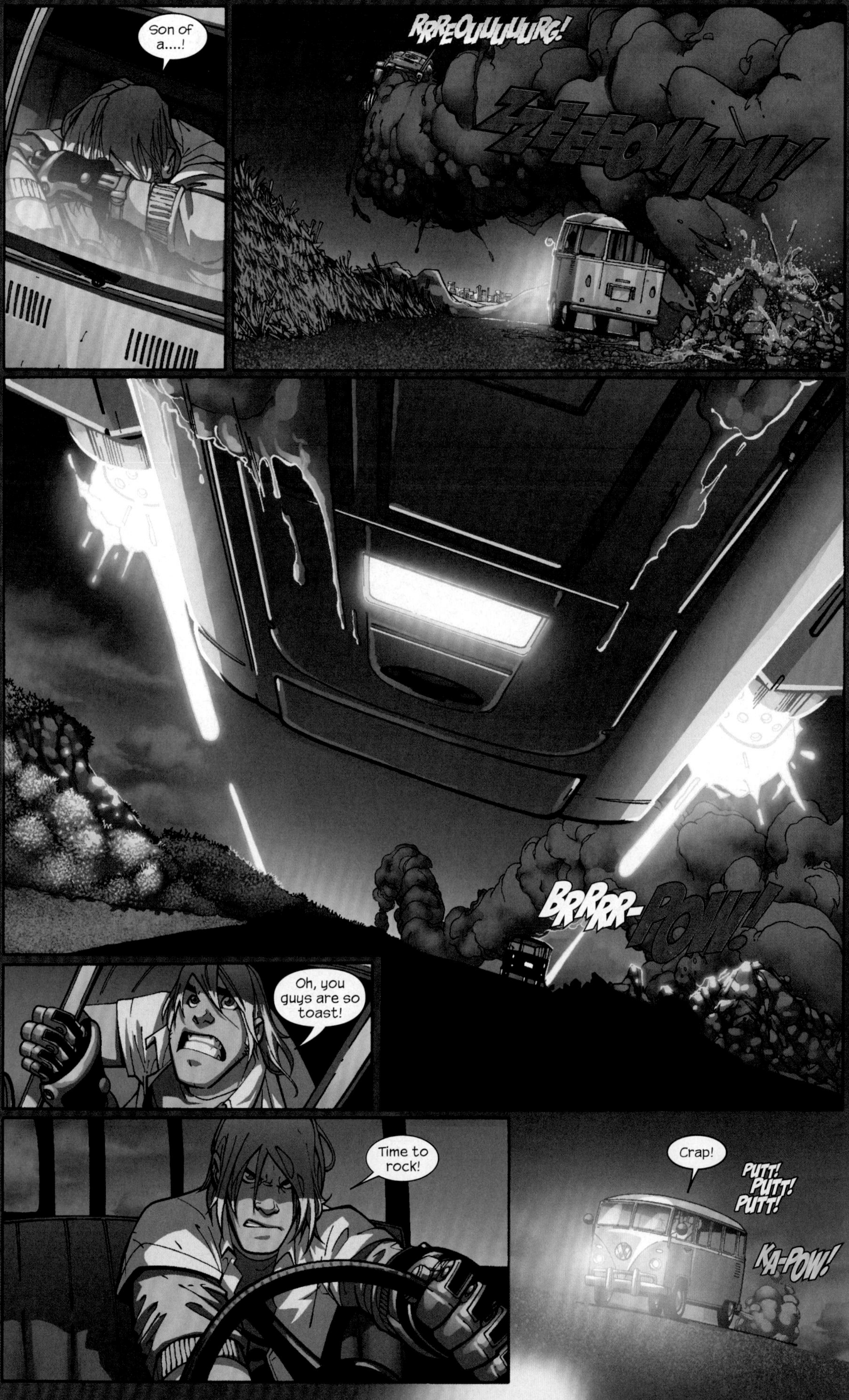
Son of a....!
RRREOUUUUURG!
ZZEEEOWWW!
BRRRR-POW!
Oh, you guys are so toast!
Time to rock!
Crap!
PUTT! PUTT! PUTT!
KA-POW!

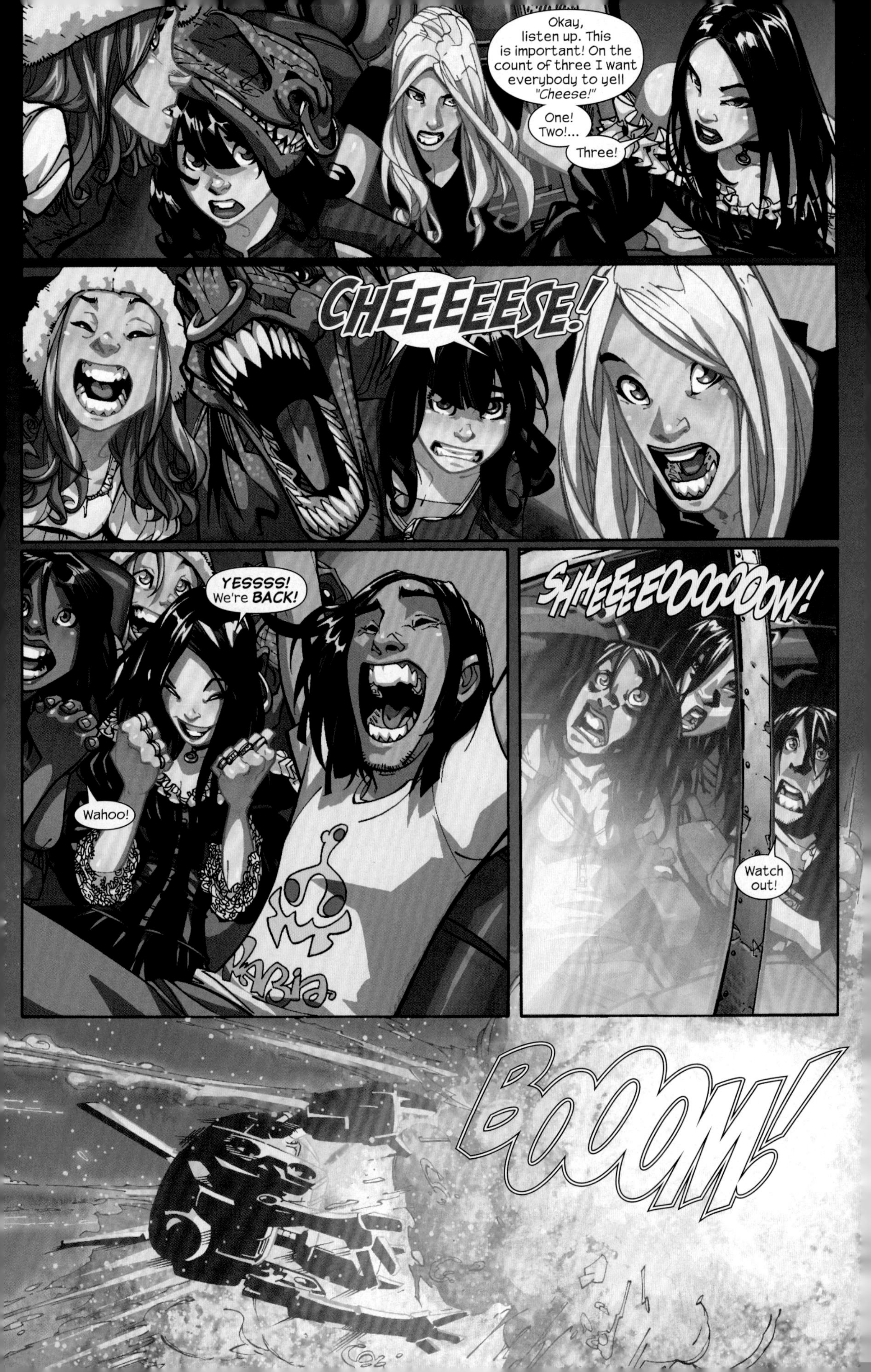
Okay, listen up. This is important! On the count of three I want everybody to yell "Cheese!"
One! Two!...
Three!
CHEEEEEESE!
YESSSS! We're BACK!
Wahoo!
SHHEEEEOOOOOOOW!
Watch out!
BOOOM!

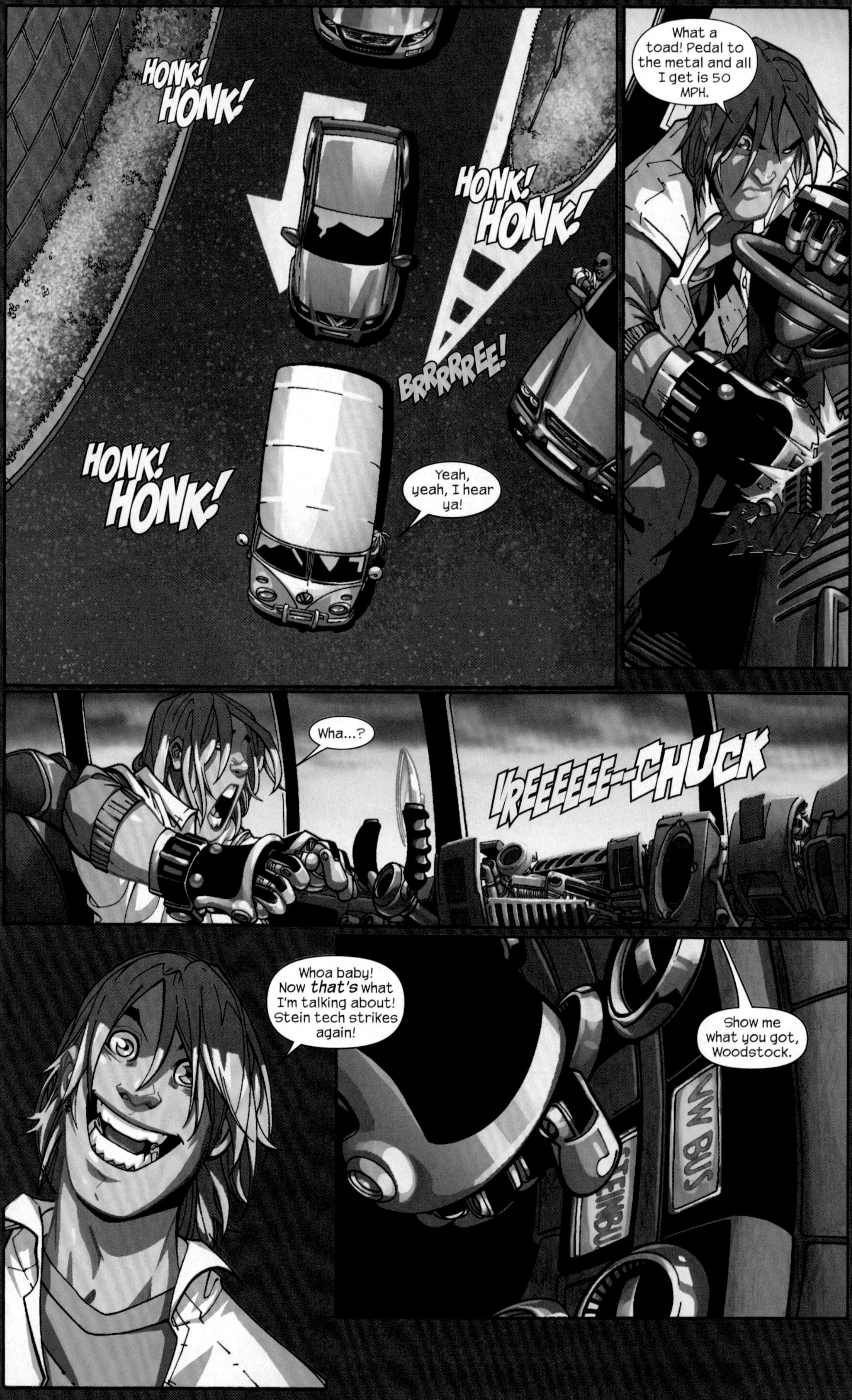
HONK! HONK!
HONK! HONK!
BRRRRREE!
HONK! HONK!
Yeah, yeah, I hear ya!
What a toad! Pedal to the metal and all I get is 50 MPH.
BAM!
Wha...?
VREEEEEE-CHUCK
Whoa baby! Now *that's* what I'm talking about! Stein tech strikes again!
Show me what you got, Woodstock.
VW BUS

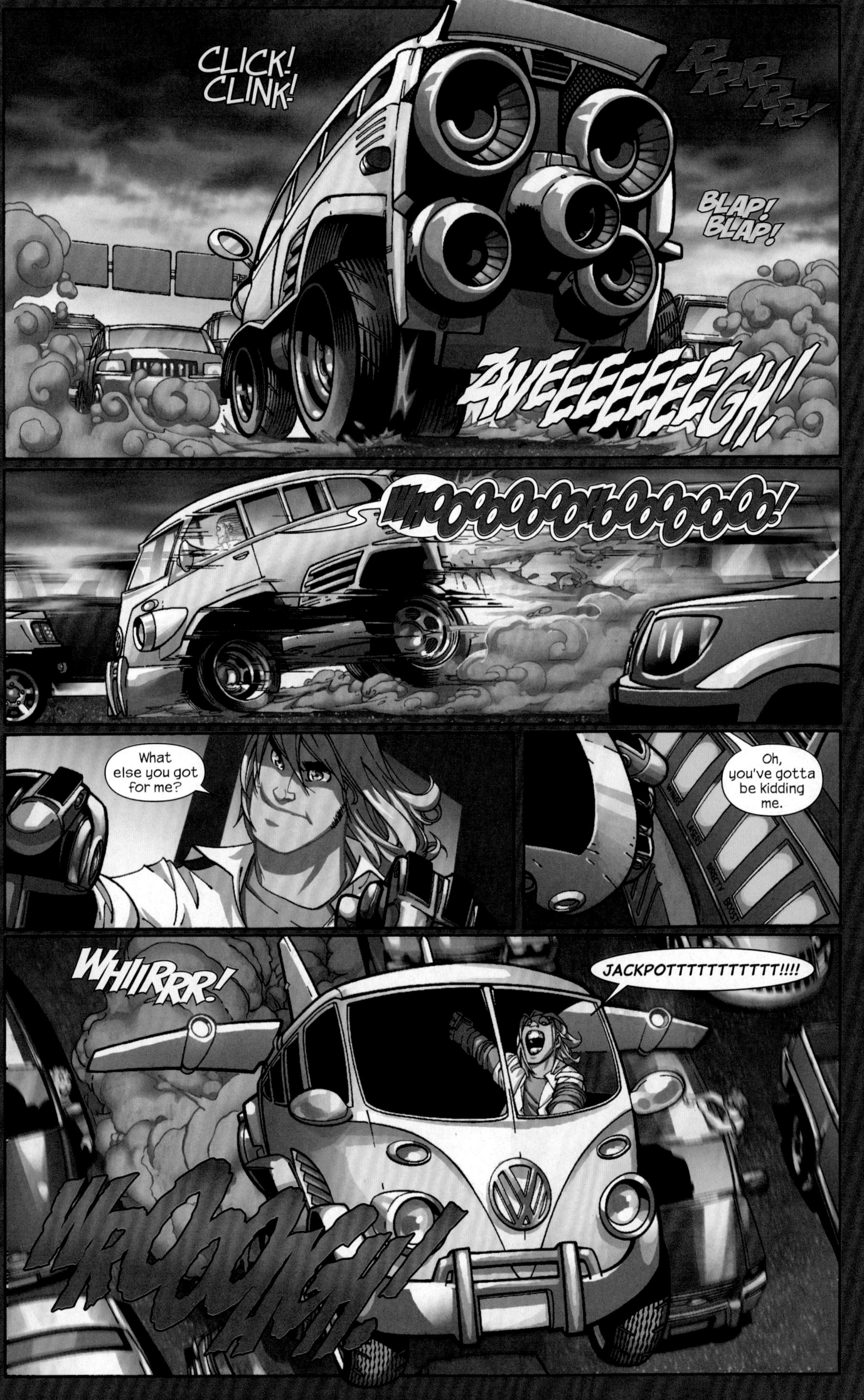
CLICK! CLINK!
BLAP! BLAP!
What else you got for me?
Oh, you've gotta be kidding me.
WHIRRR!
JACKPOTTTTTTTTTTT!!!!

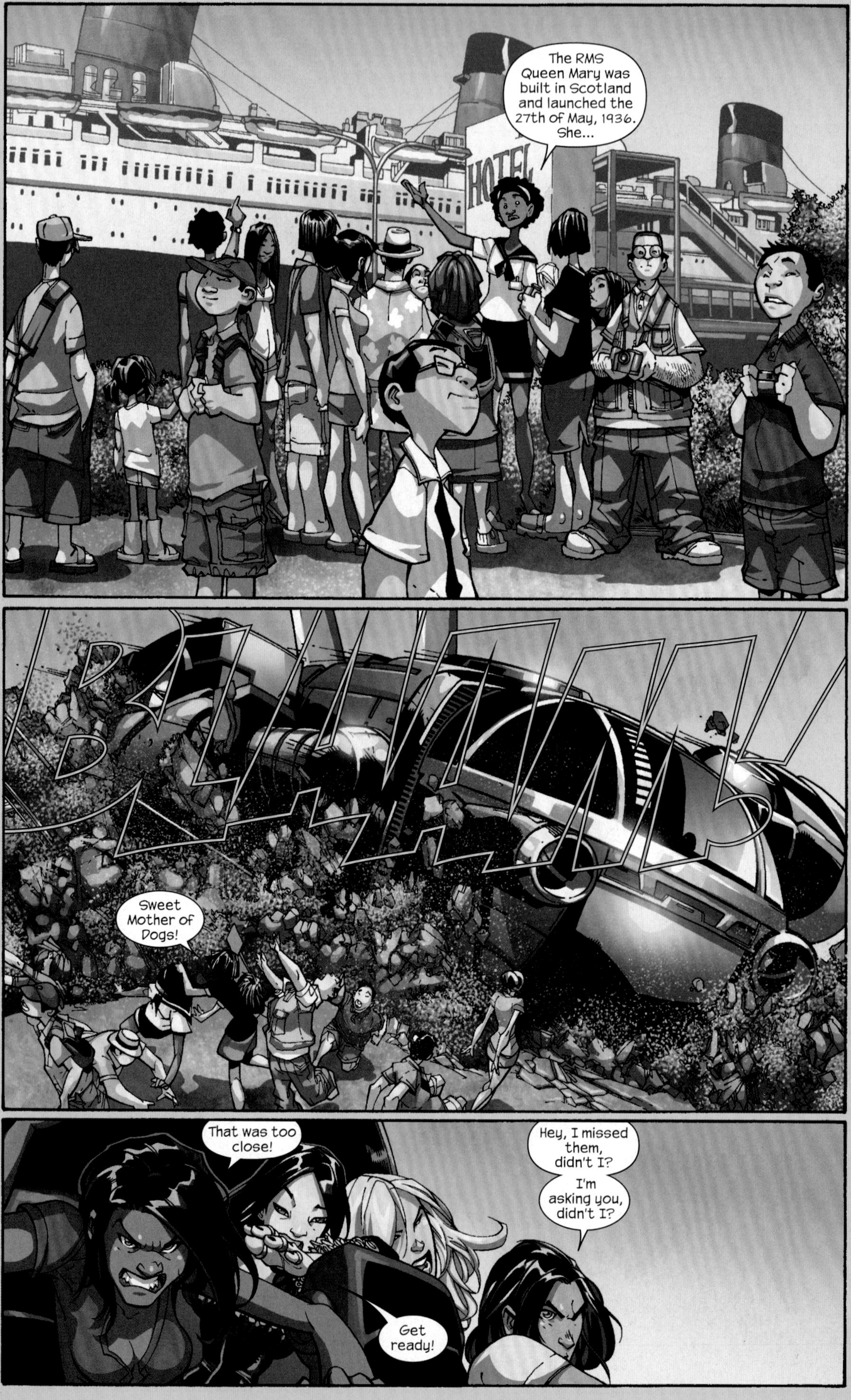
The RMS Queen Mary was built in Scotland and launched the 27th of May, 1936. She...
HOTEL
Sweet Mother of Dogs!
That was too close!
Hey, I missed them, didn't I?
I'm asking you, didn't I?
Get ready!

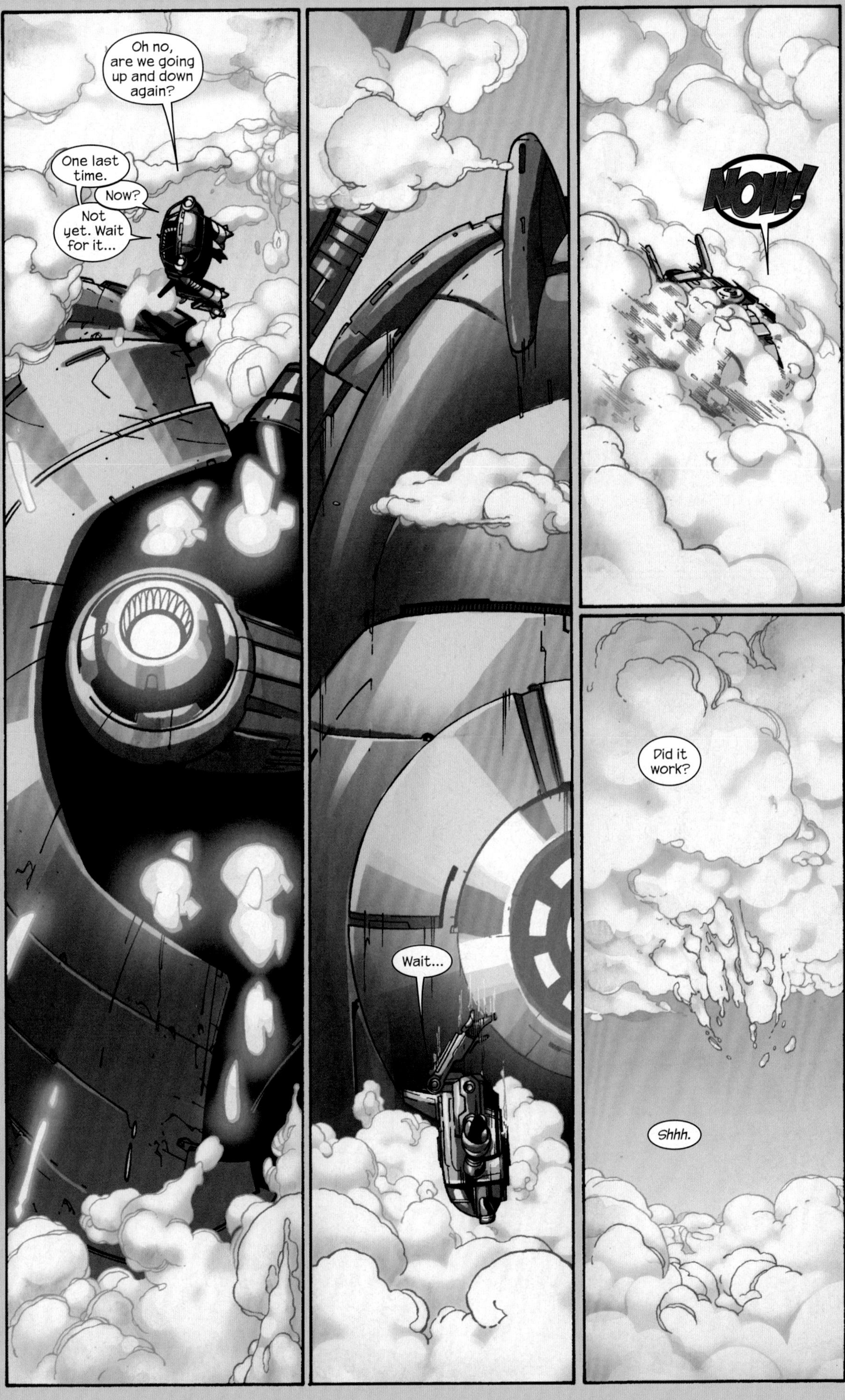
Oh no, are we going up and down again?
One last time.
Now?
Not yet. Wait for it...
Wait...
NOW!
Did it work?
Shhh.

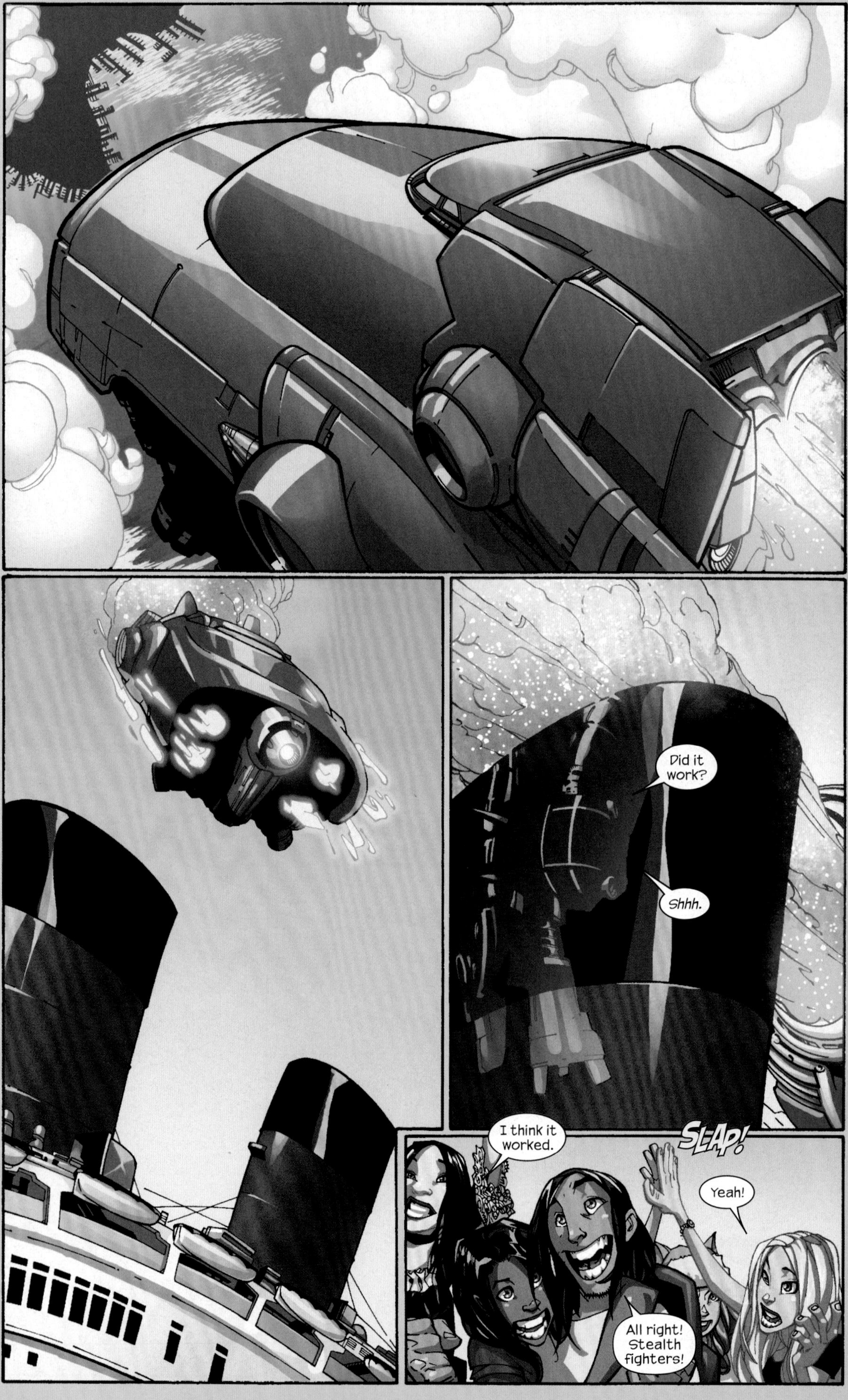
Did it work?
Shhh.
I think it worked.
SLAP!
Yeah!
All right! Stealth fighters!

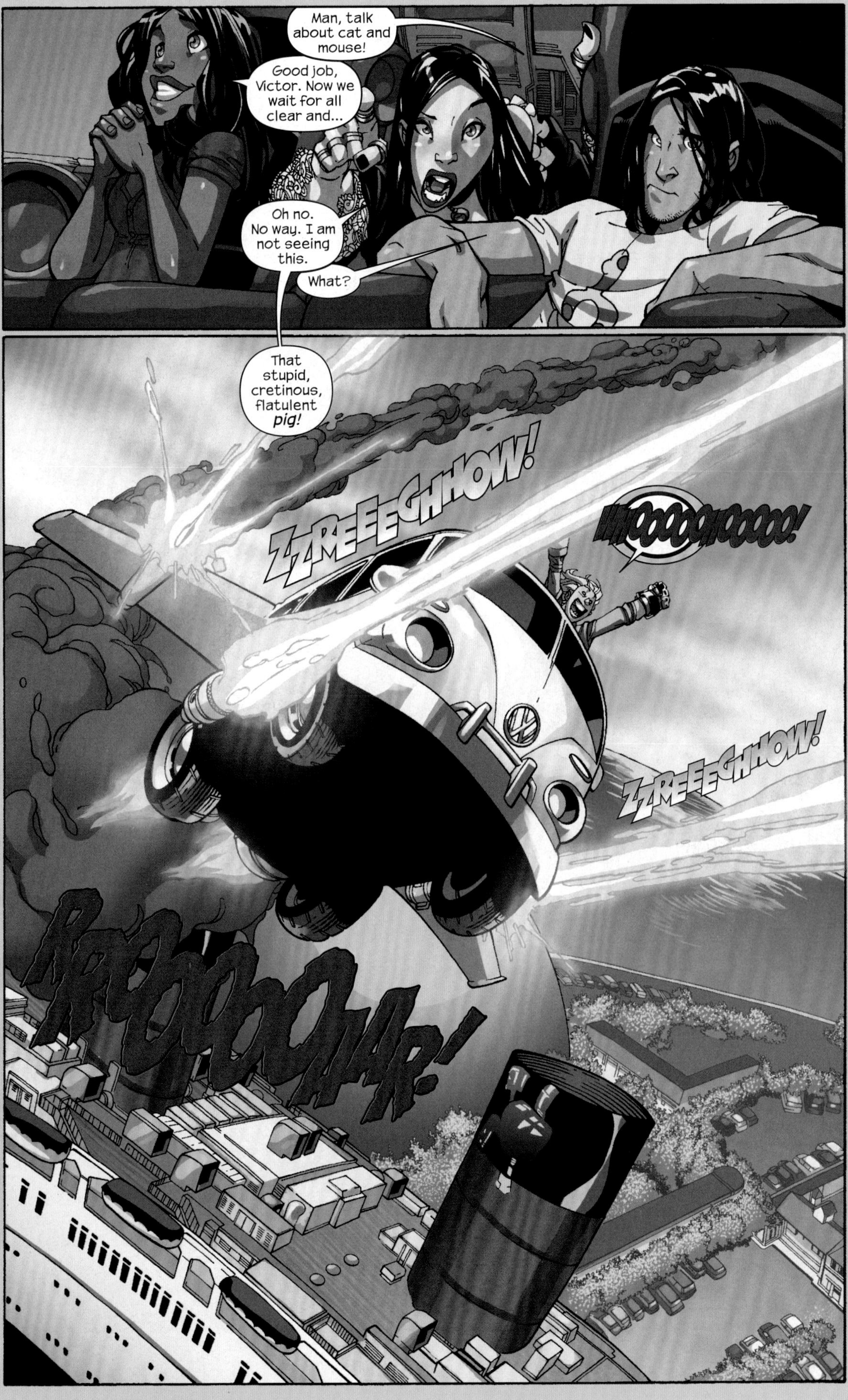
Man, talk about cat and mouse!
Good job, Victor. Now we wait for all clear and...
Oh no. No way. I am not seeing this.
What?
That stupid, cretinous, flatulent *pig!*
ZZREEEEGHHOW!
ZZREEEEGHHOW!

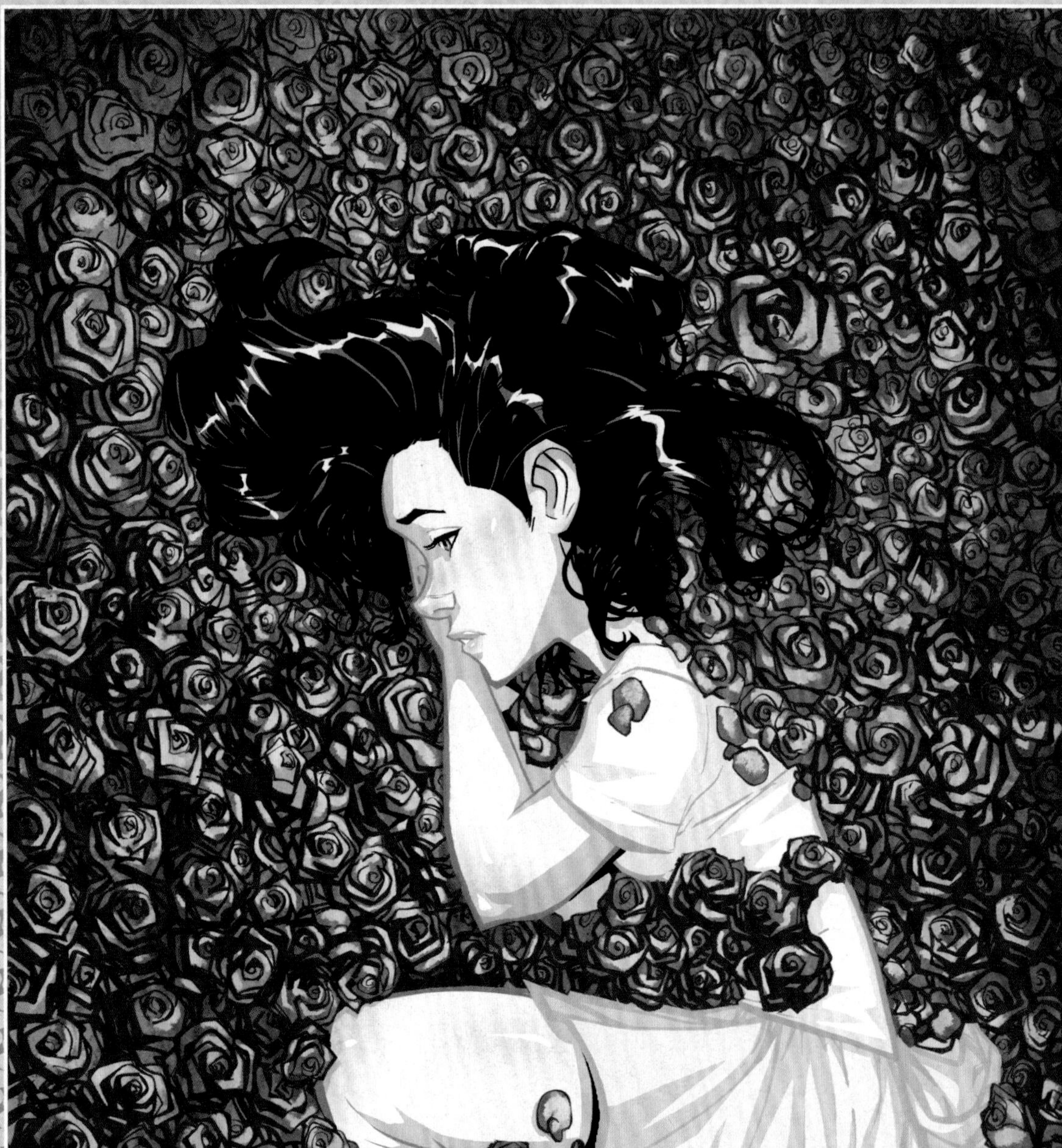
RAMOS
08
christina

6

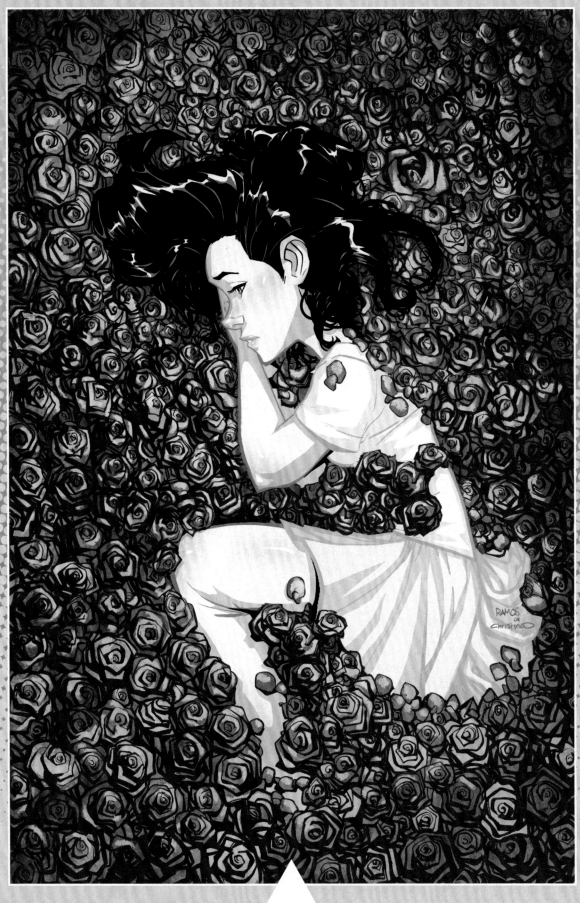

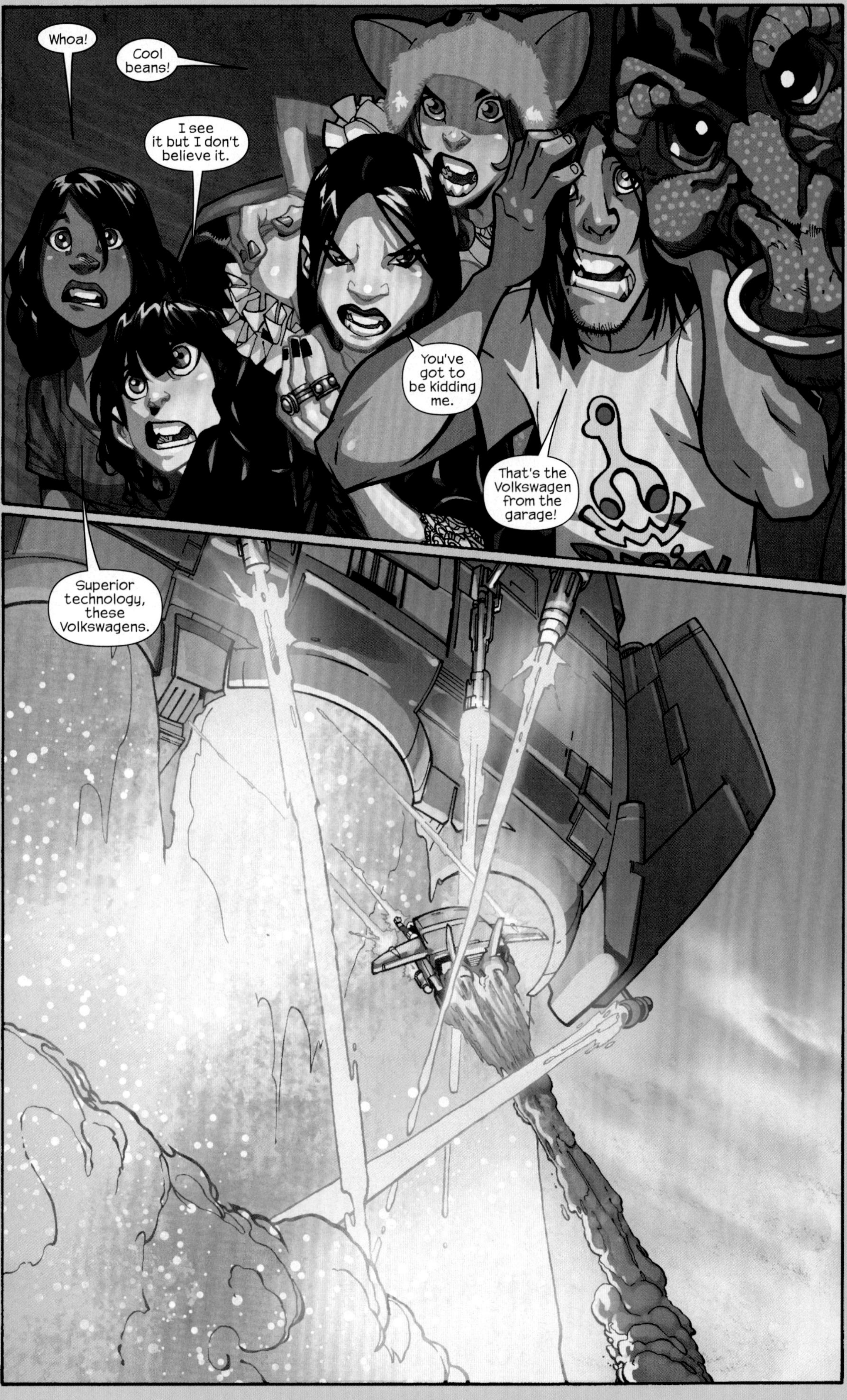
Whoa!
Cool beans!
I see it but I don't believe it.
You've got to be kidding me.
That's the Volkswagen from the garage!
Superior technology, these Volkswagens.

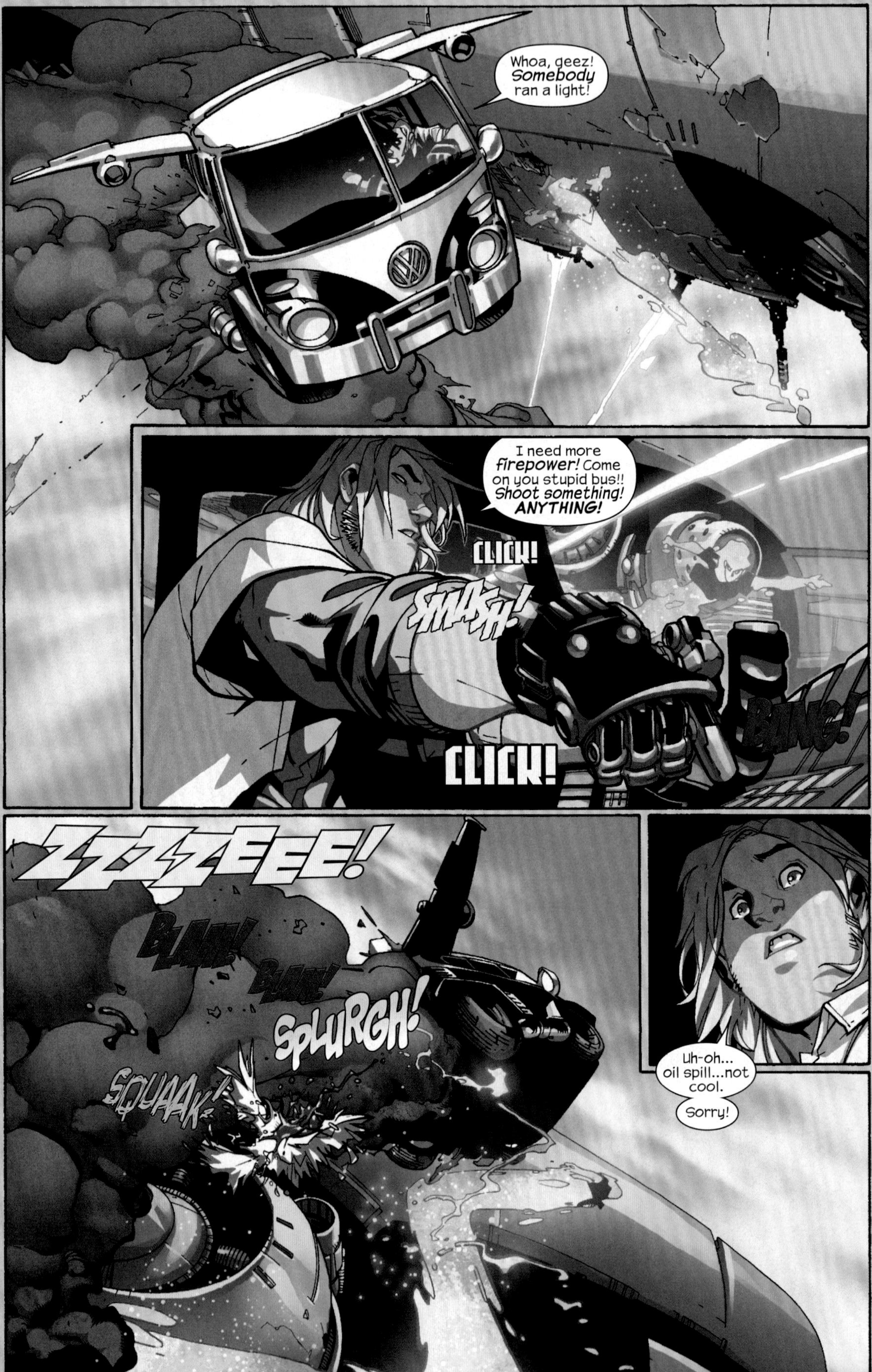
Whoa, geez! Somebody ran a light!
I need more firepower! Come on you stupid bus!! Shoot something! ANYTHING!
CLICK!
SMASH!
CLICK!
BANG!
ZZZZEEEE!
BLAM!
BLAM!
SPLURGH!
SQUAAK!
Uh-oh... oil spill...not cool.
Sorry!

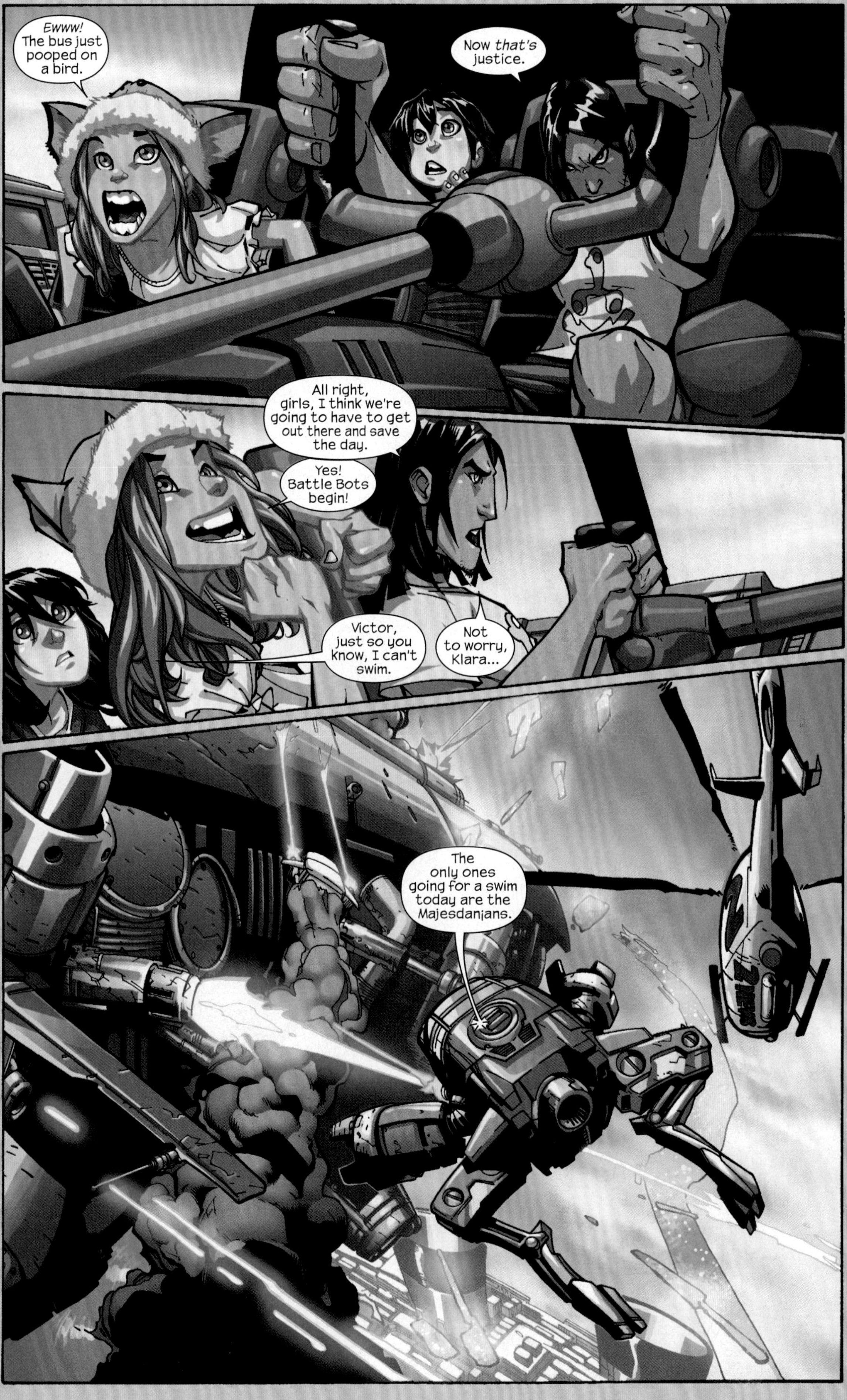
Ewww! The bus just pooped on a bird.
Now that's justice.
All right, girls, I think we're going to have to get out there and save the day.
Yes! Battle Bots begin!
Victor, just so you know, I can't swim.
Not to worry, Klara...
The only ones going for a swim today are the Majesdanians.

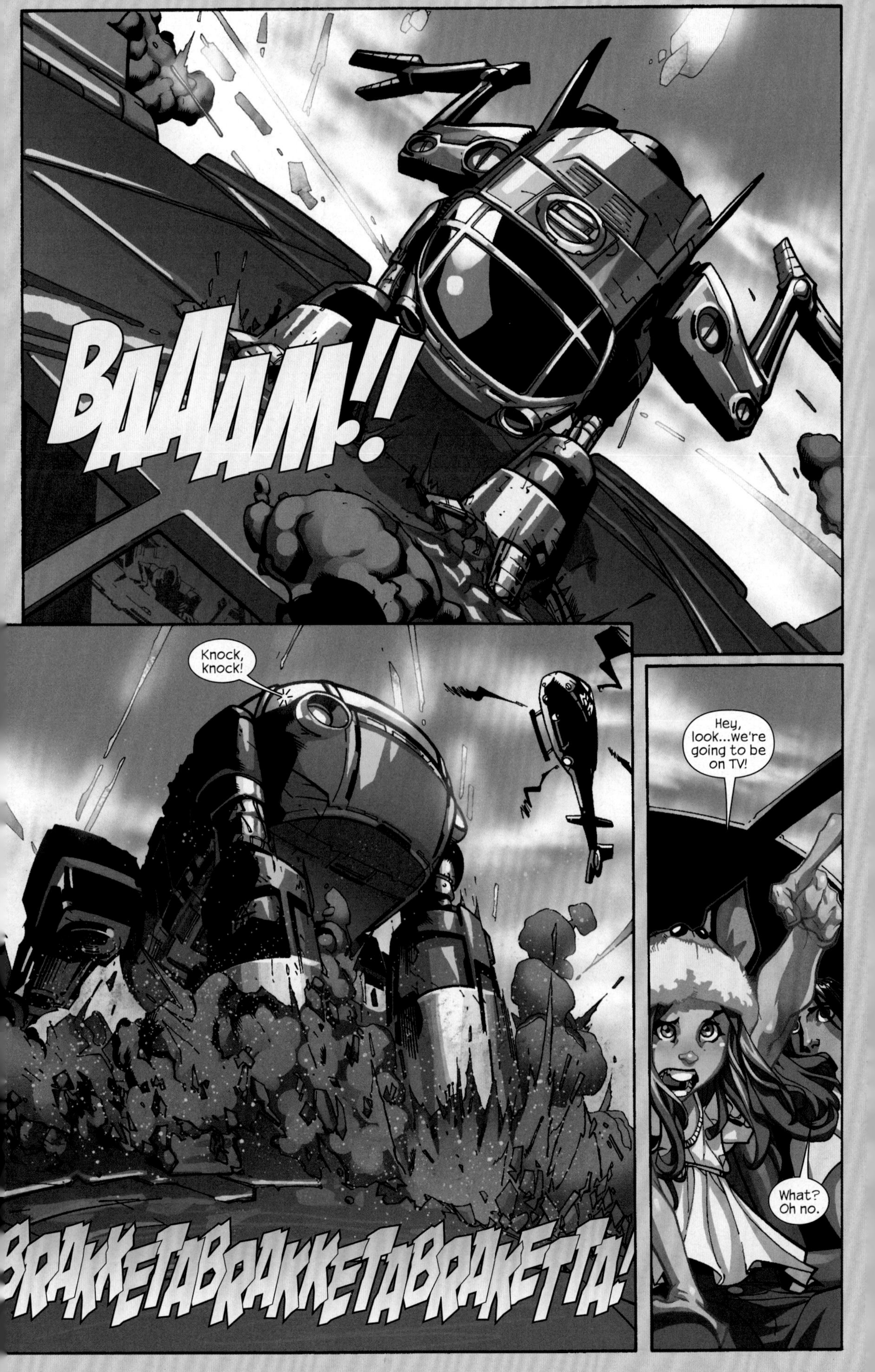
BAAAM!!
Knock, knock!
BRAKKETABRAKKETABRAKETTA!
Hey, look...we're going to be on TV!
What? Oh no.

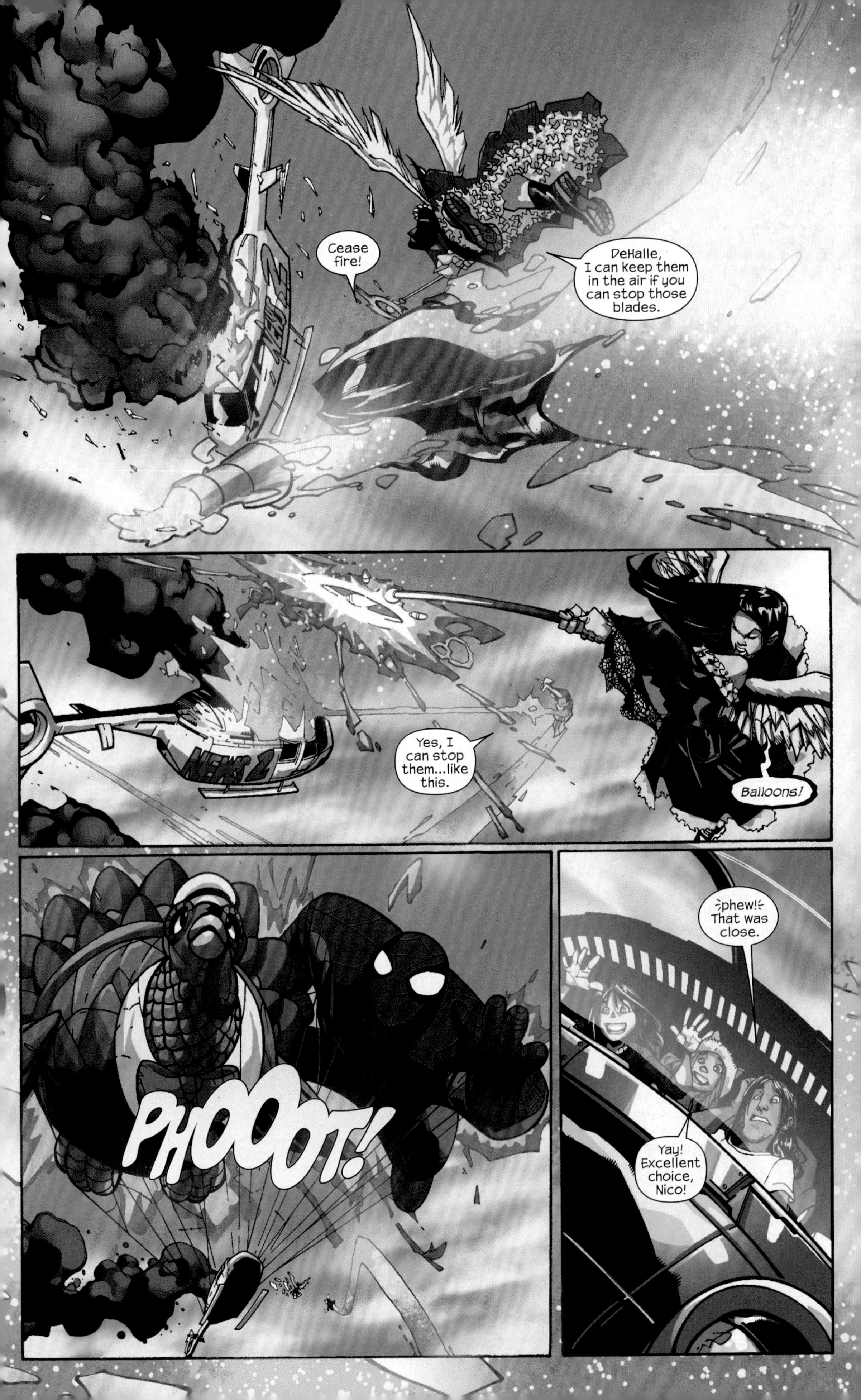
Cease fire!
DeHalle, I can keep them in the air if you can stop those blades.
Yes, I can stop them...like this.
Balloons!
PHOOOT!
-phew!- That was close.
Yay! Excellent choice, Nico!

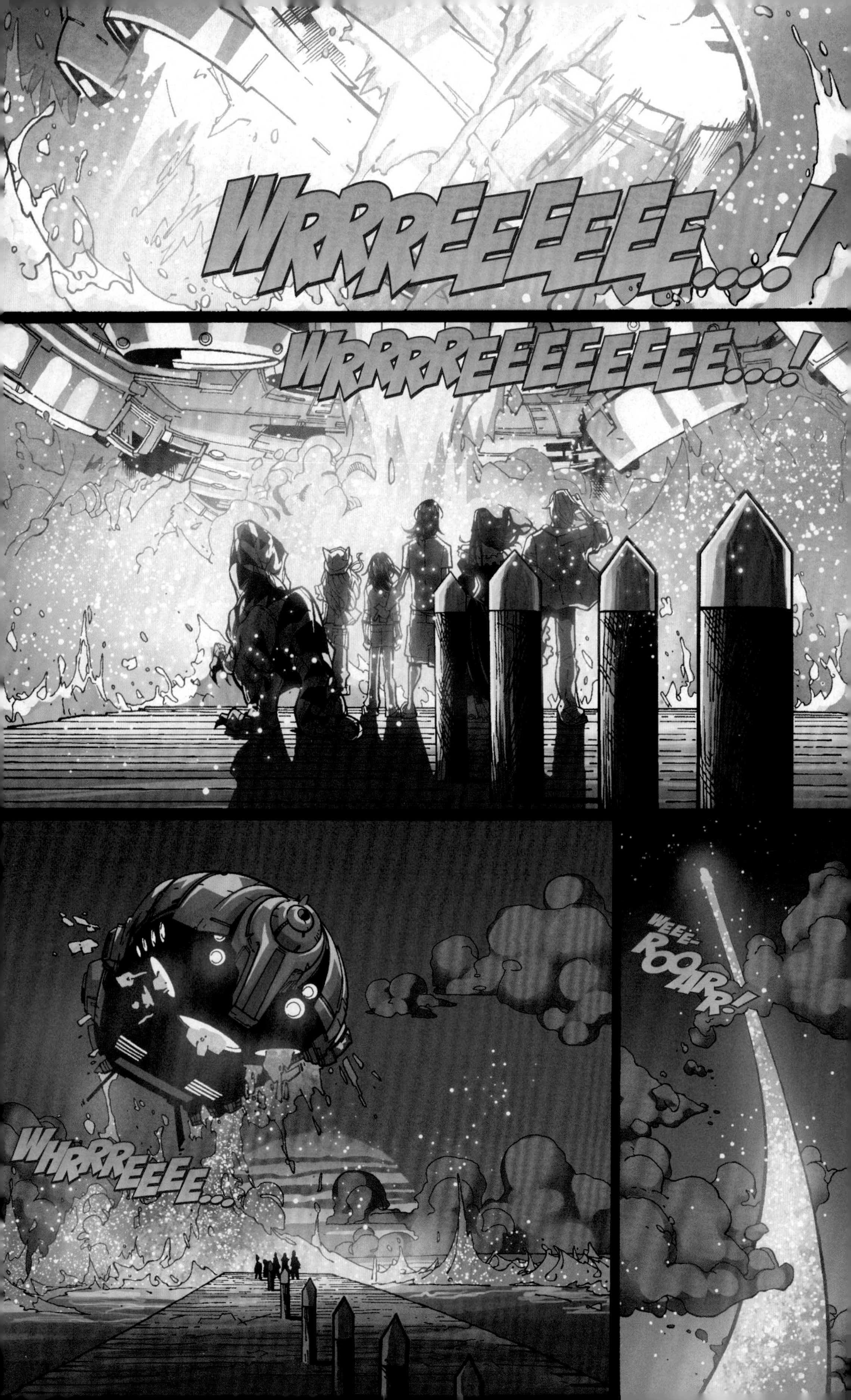
WRRREEEEEEE....!
WRRRREEEEEEEEE...!
WHRRRREEEE...
WEEE-ROOARR!

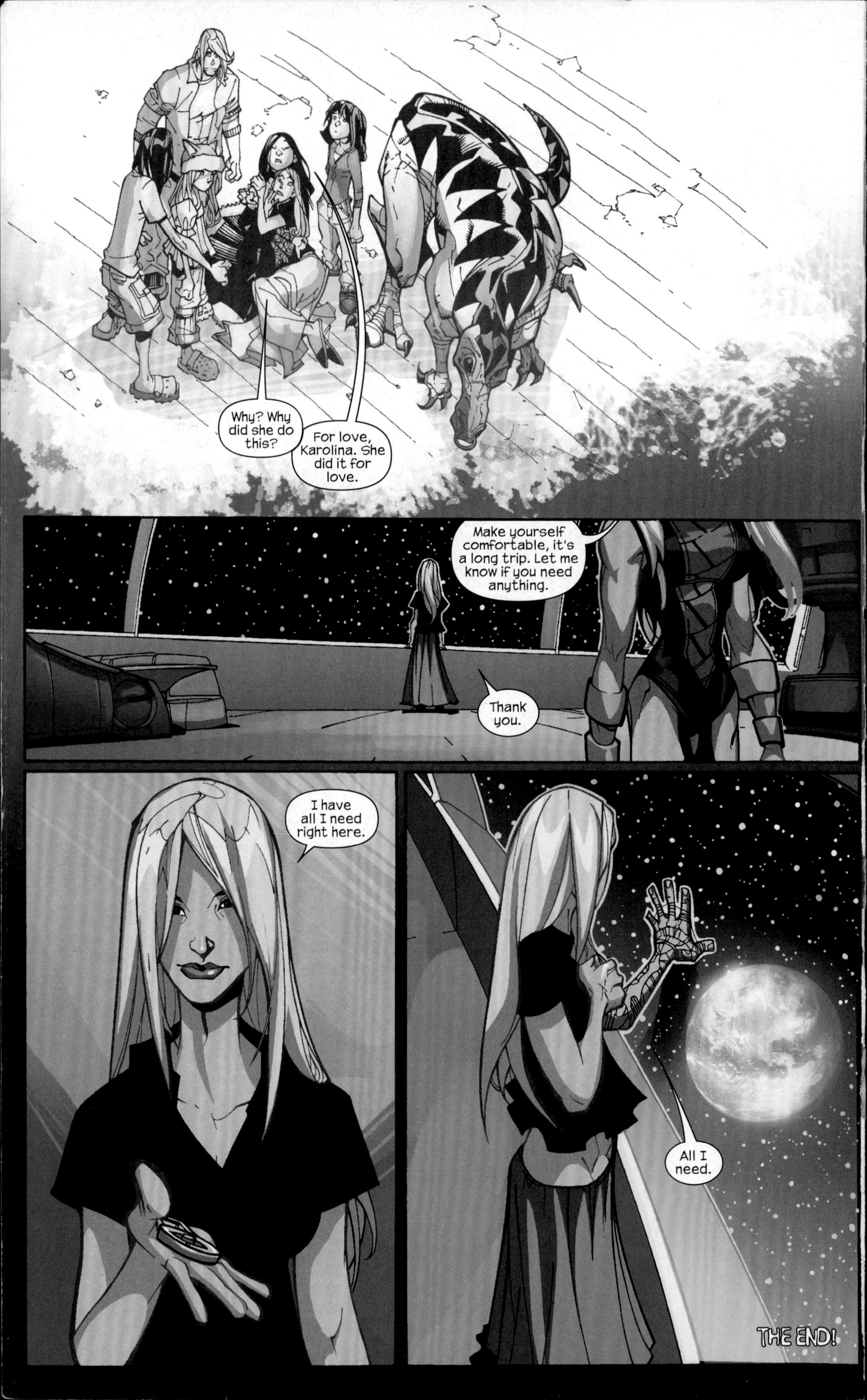
Why? Why did she do this?
For love, Karolina. She did it for love.
Make yourself comfortable, it's a long trip. Let me know if you need anything.
Thank you.
I have all I need right here.
All I need.
THE END!